THE

Playbook

HOW EMOTIONAL INTELLIGENCE RESHAPES TALENT AND PERFORMANCE

"I had the absolute pleasure of reading the first three chapters of The Talent Matrix, and it's clear this book is a transformative journey. Right from the start, it captivated me with its fresh perspective on how emotional intelligence reshapes talent management in today's fast-paced business world. Soha and Ghenwa have brilliantly combined deep insights with practical strategies, making complex ideas easy to understand and immediately applicable. Their approach to emotional intelligence as a cornerstone of talent management makes this a must-read for HR professionals and leaders alike.

What stood out to me was the genuine passion that shines through in every word. Soha and Ghenwa's commitment to helping professionals apply emotional intelligence within their organizations is both inspiring and motivating. If the first three chapters are any indication, The Talent Matrix is set to be a game-changer in the field. I highly recommend this book to anyone looking to elevate their leadership and drive impactful change in their teams and organizations."

Andrew Wolhuter, *Senior Consultant, Biz Group*

"This book offers an in-depth exploration of the challenges leaders face regarding Emotional Intelligence (EQ) and provides effective strategies for overcoming them. It serves as a valuable toolkit for leadership to drive meaningful business impact through their teams and the people they influence.

With its comprehensive, research-based, and action-oriented approach, this resource is essential for any leader, whether at the junior or senior level, seeking to make a lasting, positive difference within their organization.

What Soha and Ghenwa have achieved with this book is remarkable. It is a progressive, purposeful, and practical 'how-to' guide for leaders and professionals alike. I look forward to keeping it close at hand and benefiting regularly from Soha and Ghenwa's invaluable insights."

Anindyo Naskar, *Deputy General Manager, Learning and Development COE, Landmark Group*

"Understanding Emotional Intelligence has been a game-changer for me. The insights on self-awareness and empathy have not only improved my personal life but have also elevated my effectiveness as a leader in the workplace. I've found that integrating these concepts has led to stronger teamwork, enhanced productivity, and more meaningful connections with my colleagues. As a professional navigating a fast-paced environment, grasping the significance of Emotional Intelligence has been transformative. The understanding of intrapersonal and interpersonal intelligence will empower me to make informed decisions, manage relationships effectively, and ultimately thrive in my career. This integration is not just theoretical; it's a practical necessity for success in today's dynamic workplace."

Asli Cakir, *Vice President of Human Resources, Schneider Electric*

"I really enjoyed reading ***The Talent Matrix*** *and found it packed with practical insights on talent management that are not only informative but also easy to apply in day-to-day business. What really resonated with me were the chapters on Emotional Intelligence (EI). Having spent many years in the recruitment industry and working with people from all over the world, I've seen firsthand how crucial EI is in understanding the true needs and pain points of both candidates and clients. My ability to tap into EI has been key to my success, and this book goes beyond the typical 'soft skill' approach, emphasizing how EI can help manage stress and improve team dynamics, both of which are critical to building a positive workplace culture today.*

In short, this book is outstanding. It's not just a guide to becoming a better leader or employee but a valuable tool you'll want to keep close by to help navigate any challenges that come up with your team. I highly recommend it!"

Aws Ismail, *Co-Founder, Marc Ellis*

"For HR professionals, this book offers valuable insights into how leveraging a focus on Emotional Intelligence in your HR Architecture can support fostering a positive organizational culture and improve employee engagement. By integrating the principles outlined in this book, you can enhance your ability to navigate complex social dynamics, improve decision-making, and ultimately contribute to a more cohesive and productive work environment. This book is a must-read for any HR leader committed to transforming their organizational culture.

The Talent Matrix delves into the critical role emotional intelligence plays in our success at work, illustrating how self-awareness, empathy, and emotional regulation are the true key drivers of creating cultures that enable."

Dominic Keogh Peters, *Group CHRO, Galadari Brothers*

"If you are looking for a simple yet comprehensive and impactful guide on Emotional Intelligence and its link to contemporary Talent Management and Leadership Development, then look no further; you have reached your destination!

It is an eye-opening book combining theory and practical guidelines linking Emotional Intelligence to different elements of Talent Management including talent acquisition, retention, and future skills development. In today's business environment, it is imperative for leaders to be equipped with EI skills to manage complexities, uncertainties, and ambiguities and to build a culture of trust and performance among their teams.

This is a great book for anyone who wants to embark on a journey to develop Emotional Intelligence skills and become self-aware of their own emotions and their interactions with others around them. It provides valuable insights on how EI can play a critical role in organizations and create a positive impact in our day-to-day lives."

Eyas Qatanani, *Executive Regions HR Director for Industrial and Energy Technology at Baker Hughes*

"In our increasingly automated world, soft skills like Emotional Intelligence (EI) are becoming the differentiating factor for leaders. The Talent Matrix offers a comprehensive guide to developing and leveraging these essential skills.

Filled with practical frameworks and engaging storytelling, this book provides invaluable insights for leaders at all levels. From self-awareness to empathy and communication, The Talent Matrix equips you with the tools to build high-performing teams, foster innovation, and drive organizational success. If you're committed to personal and professional growth, this book is a must-read."

Hisham Elsaied, *Regional Head of Human Resources, MENA, Helmerich and Payne*

"As a female entrepreneur passionate about organizational culture, leadership, and employee engagement, I know how crucial emotional intelligence is for success. The Talent Matrix by Soha Chahine and Ghenwa Habbal not only emphasizes emotional intelligence but also addresses the barriers to integrating it into talent management. In today's fast-paced world, where contemporary talent management demands agility, this book provides a much-needed quantum leap in leadership strategies. By embedding emotional intelligence into talent practices, organizations can foster resilience and adaptability, setting the stage for future success.

I highly recommend this book and wish Ghenwa and Soha continued success on their journey."

Inge Van Belle, *Co-Founder of Herculean Alliance, Author, and Keynote Speaker*

"This book is a groundbreaking resource for those looking to foster a high-performance culture and thrive in an ever-changing, fast-paced world economy. With a keen understanding of how emotional awareness can transform workplace dynamics, it offers invaluable strategies for engaging and retaining the newest generation of professionals. The author's insights provide a fresh perspective on integrating emotional intelligence into leadership and team building, making it indispensable for anyone aiming to excel in today's evolving work environment. This book is a must-read for leaders, HR professionals, and anyone committed to unlocking their full potential and fostering a thriving, inclusive workplace."

Joe Lahoud, *Regional President, Kärcher, Middle East Region*

*"**The Talent Matrix**" is a groundbreaking exploration of the transformative power of emotional intelligence in HR practices and traditional talent management methodology. This book offers a fresh and insightful perspective on how emotional intelligence (EQ) can enhance not only individual performance but also elevate the overall success of teams and organizations. By delving deep into the science behind EQ, the book provides actionable strategies for HR professionals to identify, nurture, and manage talent in ways that transcend traditional metrics.*

*Packed with tips, reflections, and expert advice, **The Talent Matrix** empowers HR professionals to rethink how they assess and develop their workforce and challenge contemporary practices in a daring yet different way. Whether you're navigating complex interpersonal dynamics, fostering a culture of empathy and resilience, or optimizing employee engagement, this book is an essential guide if you dare to be different and are willing to take that leap of faith in a VUCA world.*

A must-read for anyone committed to building more emotionally intelligent, adaptive, and high-performing teams, The Talent Matrix unlocks the potential for deeper human connections to drive sustained business success."

Joe Chalouhi, *Vice President, Talent Management and Organization Development, DP World*

"It's energizing to read a book that adds practicality and dimension to the truth that emotional intelligence is a major determinant of success and leadership effectiveness, as the authors of this book so gracefully detail. The authors' refreshing and candid perspective on behaviors and a leader's ability to operate on the human side of business is a must-read for any people leader committed to the success of the people in their care, the organization in its entirety, and the firm's stakeholders. For HR professionals, this book is a valuable insight tool to help coach leaders through their growth beyond IQ and into the often-uncomfortable world of EQ development. For anyone whose work involves leading and working with people, this book can help mature the people-skill muscles that strengthen any team."

Kristofer Kumfert, *Global Human Resources Executive | Business Development Leader, Lucid Motors*

"Although you can become an engineer if you have a great IQ, you can only manage a bunch of engineers if you have a great EQ." This book is an intelligent take on a merger of Emotional Quotient & Management principles. I appreciate how Soha and Ghenwa have coupled their experiences with their perspectives. The outcome is a book that specifically merges the relationship of EQ within different domains of human resources."

Kunal Wadhwani, *CHRO, Choithrams Group*

"The Talent Matrix is one of those rare books that doesn't just talk about Emotional Intelligence—it redefines how we use it in talent management. Unlike traditional approaches that focus solely on theory, Soha Chahine and Ghenwa Habbal offer fresh, practical insights that challenge outdated methods. This book takes Emotional Intelligence beyond surface-level understanding and shows how it can be strategically applied to revolutionize leadership, team dynamics, and performance. It's a bold, forward-thinking guide that pushes boundaries and offers tools that genuinely reshape the future of talent management. If you're ready to move

beyond the ordinary and embrace a new way of thinking about EI, The Talent Matrix is your roadmap."

Maher Sabbagh, *AVP of People and Performance, Damac Group*

"The Talent Matrix is a unique resource that rethinks traditional methods of talent management and provides revolutionary approaches centered around the practical use of Emotional Intelligence. Leveraging these innovative techniques, equips leaders to navigate constant disruptions and drive meaningful, measurable results in today's dynamic and fast-changing world. Kudos to the authors whose clear explanations make complex ideas accessible to readers at any level; their remarkable knowledge and passion make it a compelling read. Whether you are new to the concepts of Emotional Intelligence and the field of managing talent or a seasoned professional, this book will undoubtedly add a fresh perspective to your work."

Nancy Zakharia Ohanessian, *Leadership Coach and Talent & Organizational Development Leader at McDermott International*

"The Talent Matrix is a transformative guide for leaders and organizations seeking sustainable success in today's complex business environment. Through a deep exploration of Emotional Intelligence (EI), the book emphasizes how crucial self-awareness, empathy, and emotional resilience are for driving effective leadership, fostering teamwork, and navigating change. Drawing on research and real-world examples, it highlights the vital role EI plays in talent management, organizational culture, and performance.

This is a must-read for any leader or professional aiming to build emotionally intelligent teams that can thrive in an unpredictable, fast-paced world. The insights provided are not only practical but also essential for those who aspire to create a more empathetic, resilient, and high-performing organization."

Najib Makarem, *Group Chief Human Resources Officer, National Holding*

"This book offers a rich, well-rounded exploration of how Emotional Intelligence (EI) can revolutionize talent management and organizational success. Written by seasoned HR professionals, "The Talent Matrix" provides a practical roadmap for integrating EI into various aspects of talent management, from recruitment to leadership development. As an ICF coach, this text is particularly valuable. It not only reinforces key coaching principles—like empathy, self-awareness, and resilience—but also presents actionable strategies for fostering these traits within teams. The authors blend personal experience with contemporary HR practices, making it both relatable and insightful. Its focus on adapting to the VUCA (volatile, uncertain, complex, and ambiguous) world through EI resonates deeply with coaching frameworks.

For HR leaders or coaches seeking to create emotionally intelligent, resilient teams, this book is an essential read. It bridges theory with practice, empowering professionals to drive meaningful, people-centered transformation."

Nic Woodthorpe-Wright, *Managing Director, WWA Corporate Coaching*

"'The Talent Matrix: How Emotional Intelligence Reshapes Talent and Performance' by Ghenwa Habbal and Soha Chahine is a must-read for HR professionals and business leaders navigating today's complex and rapidly changing work environment. This insightful playbook comprehensively explores how Emotional Intelligence (EI) can be leveraged to drive talent management and enhance performance. It is filled with practical strategies and actionable insights on integrating EI into various facets of HR, from talent acquisition and conflict resolution to leadership and performance management.

I admire the depth and authenticity that both authors bring to this work. Their real-world experiences and forward-thinking approaches offer a fresh perspective on building resilient organizations. "The Talent Matrix" stands out as a powerful guide to fostering emotional intelligence in the workplace, providing tools to create dynamic, adaptable, and high-performing teams. Highly recommended for anyone committed to developing talent with a human touch."

Pamela Xaba, *Founding Member – Nonkosi Creatives HR Consultancy*

"The Talent Matrix is a groundbreaking playbook for HR professionals, business leaders, and anyone involved in organizational development. Chahine and Habbal masterfully show how emotional intelligence can transform not only individuals but entire organizations, making it an indispensable resource for creating emotionally intelligent, adaptable, and high-performing teams. The insights provided are timely and crucial for thriving in today's dynamic corporate landscape, and the practical tools offered make the book an essential guide for implementing change that leads to sustainable success."

Saad El Hage, PhD, *Regional Director - Middle East and Africa, Headspring*

"The Talent Matrix by Soha Chahine and Ghenwa Habbal is a thoughtful read for people working in corporates, skillfully demystifying the linkage and impact of EI in various HR processes as well as in the leadership roles.

This engaging piece of work provides insights into the role of Emotional Intelligence and how it can help us succeed in real-life situations. A recommended read!"

Sarma Chillara, *CHRO, Volkswagen Group – Region India*

"Practitioners Soha Chahine and Ghenwa Habbal are just like you. Their daily work centers on partnering with organizations facing conditions beyond their control: new generations entering the workforce, technology, social media, and employee health, safety, and happiness.

These shifting conditions put pressure on noise and develop the flexibility to manage daily pressure, communicate clearly through the competing noise, and connect with others on a human level. In today's world, leaders who remain subject matter experts and not people experts will eventually derail. Performers who achieve the best top-line results but lack the EQ skills to connect, coach, and inspire others will cost organizations in turnover, drama, poor change management, and low team engagement.

More than academic theory, The Talent Matrix is a practical "how to" guide. Pick it up, turn to any chapter, and find valuable instruction to address the people-side of leadership at every stage of talent management."

Susan Clarine, *Founder and Emotional Intelligence Executive Coach, The Ei Coach, LLC*

THE TALENT MATRIX
Playbook

HOW EMOTIONAL INTELLIGENCE RESHAPES TALENT AND PERFORMANCE

DR. SOHA CHAHINE | DR. GHENWA HABBAL

GLOBAL INFLUENCERS PUBLISHING HOUSE
152 Prince Charles Cr, #17-12 Singapore 159013
Website: www.globalinfluencers.sg
Email: shikha@globalinfluencers.sg
First Published in Singapore by Global Influencers Publishing House 2024

Title: The Talent Matrix: How Emotional Intelligence Reshapes Talent and Performance (Playbook)
ISBN: Paperback 978-981-94-1697-4/ Kindle 978-981-94-1698-1

GLOBAL INFLUENCERS PUBLISHING HOUSE

Dedications

To fellow entrepreneurs and startup leaders
weaving innovation with empathy:
This venture is for you.

To fellow visionary CHROs and business leaders
balancing strategic acumen with a human touch:
This opus is for you.

To fellow dedicated HR professionals, the
backbone of workplace culture and employee
engagement:
This companion is for you.

To fellow future HR Shapers of the workplace:
This is fuel for you.

To our families, who are the lighthouse and our
forever inspiration:
This book is for you.

CONTENTS

FOREWORD

Dr. Hannah Haikal

HR Director, Europe, Africa, Middle East, & Eurasia Distribution - Caterpillar

What if the real breakthrough in building a high-performing workforce isn't about the latest technologies or another change program but in recalibrating our approach to human interaction? In a world where data and technology dominate, could the most profound driver of organizational success be our ability to connect on a human level? ***The Talent Matrix*** by Dr. Soha Chahine and Dr. Ghenwa Habbal explores this notion by positioning Emotional Intelligence (EI) not just as a leadership skill but as the cornerstone for transforming every stage of the talent lifecycle—from hiring and talent development to conflict resolution and performance management. With practical strategies grounded in real-world application, this book empowers leaders and HR professionals to build stronger, more adaptive organizations that thrive in today's complex workplace.

I've had the privilege of collaborating with Soha and Ghenwa through HR networks and conferences, as well as having plenty of insightful chats over coffee! What impressed me most, beyond their clear expertise, was their natural ability to connect with others on a personal level, whether speaking to a room full of professionals or engaging in one-on-one conversations. It's clear that they don't just teach EI—they live it, and that experience shines through in this body of work.

What sets this book apart is its ability to bring together the latest research on EI and demonstrate its practical implications for modern talent management. Traditionally, EI has been seen primarily as a tool for handling emotions and boosting leadership skills. While these aspects are important, ***The Talent Matrix*** broadens this view by presenting EI as a crucial component across every facet of talent management and demonstrates tangible ways to apply theory in practice.

While Intelligence Quotient (IQ) has been the benchmark for measuring cognitive abilities and academic success, this book flips the script by showing how a deeper, more practical approach to EI can drive meaningful change. It emphasizes that EI is not just an innate trait but a skill that can be developed and refined over time. This perspective is especially relevant in a data-driven world where metrics often overshadow the human elements of work.

In my career, I've seen how leaders who prioritize EI are able to cultivate stronger, more cohesive teams. Leaders who understand and manage emotions, both their own and those of their teams, create an environment where people feel empowered, engaged, and motivated to contribute their best. I recall a time when I was coaching a leader through a challenging project. The team was struggling with communication breakdowns and unresolved conflicts, and performance was taking a hit. Although I didn't have access to ***The Talent Matrix*** at the time, I drew on key EI principles—empathy, active listening, and open dialogue. I guided the leader in holding sessions focused on resolving these conflicts and understanding emotional triggers. As the team began to engage in these conversations, their interactions improved, performance metrics rose, and cohesion strengthened. This experience highlights how EI as a *shared strength* can transform team dynamics and drive results, a point that ***The Talent Matrix*** explores in depth.

The Talent Matrix also sets out recommendations for how to manage conflict constructively, navigate complex interpersonal relationships, and lead through change—all crucial in today's fast-paced work environments. By offering practical solutions to these common issues, this book equips readers with the knowledge and skills needed to foster a more resilient and adaptable workforce.

In closing, ***The Talent Matrix*** is more than just another guide to EI. It is a blueprint for revolutionizing how we lead, manage, and grow teams in the modern workplace. It offers fresh perspectives on integrating EI into every aspect of talent management. Whether you're a seasoned leader, an HR professional, or someone interested in personal development, this read provides valuable insights that can drive both personal growth and organizational excellence. I am confident that readers will find it as valuable and impactful as I have.

Dr. Hannah Haikal is a global HR leader and organizational psychologist with over 20 years of experience driving business transformation through progressive talent and culture practices. She has earned a reputation as a thought leader and trusted advisor to executive teams, helping to build high-performing organizations that thrive in today's dynamic environment.

ABOUT THE AUTHORS

Dr. Soha Chahine

With over 15 years of expertise in Human Resources, Dr. Soha Chahine is an Organizational Psychologist, the founder of Forward Training and Consulting, and an adjunct lecturer in management. Renowned for her creative and forward-thinking strategies, Dr. Chahine specializes in crafting ecosystems where leaders drive innovation, foster inclusivity, and navigate change with agility; where teams flourish through collaboration and adaptability; and where workplaces embody purpose, flexibility, and a culture of continuous learning, grounded in the principles of Positive Psychology and Neuroscience.

A certified EQ-i 2.0 and 360 practitioner, among other psychometric tools, Dr. Chahine applies evidence-based strategies in Emotional Intelligence, Resilience at Work, and Leadership Development to cultivate workplace cultures that adapt to change and foster sustainable innovation.

Dr. Chahine's multifaceted career spans roles as a psychometric assessor, coach, trainer, moderator, author, and award judge. A keynote speaker and a valued contributor to leading publications such as Harvard Business Review Arabia, her insights continue to shape the evolving landscape of leadership and workplace transformation, solidifying her reputation as a transformative thought leader.

You can connect with Dr. Soha at:

LinkedIn: https://www.linkedin.com/in/sohachahine/

Dr. Ghenwa Habbal

Is a global Talent Management, Employee Experience, and Change Management Leader with 20 years of expertise in building agile, high-performing, and resilient teams that drive organizational excellence.

The Creator of the F.A.S.T Model, a modern leadership framework, a multi-award-winning People & Culture Leader, Business and Industrial Psychologist, and certified Resilience and Brain-Based Coach, Dr. Habbal blends strategic foresight with hands-on expertise to deliver transformative human capital solutions.

Drawing on her cumulative knowledge in neuroscience, human psychology and psychometrics, as well as organizational psychology, Dr. Habbal specializes in fostering economies of learning where leaders innovate, teams thrive, and businesses achieve sustainable success.

Her innovative approaches to talent management, change management, and culture transformation are rooted in evidence-based methodologies that yield measurable results.

Dr. Habbal is also a respected guest lecturer, bridging academia with business industries equipping future professionals with the skills to navigate dynamic corporate landscapes. Her published articles on strategies to thrive in VUCA environments provide actionable insights for professionals and organizations seeking success.

With a proven track record of leading organizations through VUCA environments, Dr. Habbal creates psychologically safe, adaptable workplaces aligned with DEI and ESG principles. Her expertise inspires leadership transformation and fosters innovation, ensuring organizations flourish in a rapidly evolving world.

You can connect with Dr. Ghenwa at:
LinkedIn: https://www.linkedin.com/in/ghenwa-habbal/

INTRODUCTION

If you're the type who usually skips introductions, we kindly ask you to pause and give this one a read. Why? Because this book isn't just another discussion on the transformative power of Emotional Intelligence (EI) in today's workplace. It's a practical guide, filled with hands-on strategies at the intersection of Emotional Intelligence and Talent Management, designed to empower you—whether you're a Human Resources (HR) or Learning and Development Specialist, Talent Manager, Chief human resources officer (CHRO), a Leader, or a Senior Leader. These insights will equip you with the tools to harness Emotional Intelligence, enhance team dynamics, strengthen leadership, and build resilient organizations in a world that's volatile, uncertain, complex, and ambiguous (VUCA). **So buckle up, as this transformative journey is just beginning.**

In a world dominated by the unpredictable and ever-changing nature of VUCA, the landscape of talent management is evolving in real-time. The days of static performance metrics and rigid talent development methodologies are long gone. Today, we embrace a more nuanced, holistic approach with Emotional Intelligence (EI) at its core—a powerful yet often underestimated force in driving professional success.

"***The Talent Matrix***" is more than just a book! It's a pioneering exploration into how Emotional Intelligence, when strategically applied through frameworks, like the 9-Box Grid, can redefine talent management and supercharge workplace performance (Bersin, 2013). This book is your all-in-one resource, offering actionable strategies to leverage EI for enhancing performance, team dynamics, leadership qualities, and the overall health of your organization.

As you turn these pages, you'll discover that Emotional Intelligence is far from a 'soft skill' reserved for leadership retreats or team-building exercises. Instead, it's a critical asset in our VUCA world, where adaptability and resilience are key to thriving. By integrating Emotional Intelligence into every facet of talent management—from talent acquisition and conflict resolution to performance management and leadership development—you'll be equipped to create environments that don't just survive challenges but rise above them.

THE JOURNEY BEHIND THE PAGES

Our journey to creating this book was born in the trenches of the corporate world, shaped by the volatility and uncertainty that define our times. As colleagues and co-authors, we've navigated personal and professional challenges together, emerging with a deep understanding of how Emotional Intelligence (EI) can reshape talent and drive performance.

Meet Dr. Soha Chahine

Every journey begins with a single step, but mine started as a temporary background screener associate—an entry-level role that was far from glamorous but rich in lessons. It was here that I first began to climb the corporate ladder, rung by rung. Each promotion—from full-time team leader to operations manager and eventually a shareholder—was not just a career milestone but a profound lesson in leadership, resilience, and the transformative power of Emotional Intelligence (EI). The higher I climbed, the more I realized that success wasn't merely about intelligence or hard work; it was about understanding people, navigating emotions, and leading with empathy.

The corporate world, however, is rarely smooth sailing. My path took me to a Fortune 500 company, where I served in a Human Resources role during a merger and acquisition—a time fraught with uncertainty, job insecurity, and the constant fear of instability. I found myself in a storm, but instead of succumbing to the fear, I anchored myself with my EI skills—managing stress, maintaining optimism, and continuing to pursue self-actualization. These skills, alongside navigating complex interpersonal dynamics, were not just survival tactics; they were the very tools that helped me thrive amidst chaos.

But the storm was far from over. My next chapter led me to another multinational company, this time grappling with the aftermath of bankruptcy. Although I managed to hold onto my job, the sense of insecurity was ever-present, lurking like a shadow. Just when I thought the worst was behind me, the world was hit by the COVID-19 pandemic. Overnight, the security I had fought so hard to maintain was stripped away, leaving me jobless and at a crossroads.

But here's where the story takes a turn. Rather than seeing this as an end, I saw it as a new beginning—a chance to redefine my path. With over 15 years of experience in managing teams and Human Resources Management, I took this setback and transformed it into a stepping stone. I became a certified professional coach, gained several psychometric assessments, including but not limited to EQ-i 2.0 and 360-degree, and founded my own company, Forward Training and Consulting, in the UAE. But this was more than just a business venture; it was a mission, a commitment to fostering Emotional Intelligence, leadership, and resilience in others.

Why did I choose this path? I recognized early on that Emotional Intelligence was not just a nice-to-have skill but a critical component for thriving in the future of work, especially in our volatile, uncertain, complex, and ambiguous (VUCA) world. Technical skills alone were no longer enough. We needed leaders who could navigate change with empathy, resilience, and emotional intelligence. We needed employees who could adapt, collaborate, and drive innovation. We needed organizations that could cultivate a culture of Emotional Intelligence, enhancing team dynamics, leadership qualities, and overall organizational health.

My Transformation with Emotional Intelligence

The turning point came when I not only encountered Emotional Intelligence as a concept but took the EQ-i 2.0 assessment myself, becoming certified in the process. It was nothing short of a revelation. For the first time, I saw clearly how my emotions shaped my reactions and decisions. I learned to manage my feelings with greater finesse, to respond thoughtfully rather than react impulsively, and to navigate life's challenges with a newfound resilience and adaptability. This wasn't just a professional transformation; it was a personal one. The deeper understanding of Emotional Intelligence gave me a renewed sense of purpose and confidence that propelled me forward, guiding both my leadership journey and my mission to foster these skills in others.

Crossing Paths with Ghenwa Habbal

It was during this transformative period that I crossed paths with Ghenwa Habbal, a talent lead for a Fortune 500 company and a certified coach. Our meeting was serendipitous—we quickly realized that we shared a common vision. We both believed in the power of Emotional Intelligence to navigate the complexities of the VUCA world. We understood that beyond technical expertise, success in the modern workplace required a deep, practical understanding of Emotional Intelligence. Together, we set out to combine our experiences and insights in Talent Management to help others not just survive but thrive in this ever-changing landscape.

Meet Dr. Ghenwa Habbal

My professional journey began early in my teens. Between studying and working at the same time for various industries, I experienced a plethora of emotions at every stage in my career.

In the realm of Human Resources, my career spans approximately two decades.

I started as a Personnel Officer at a homegrown organization that went global. I quickly rose through the leadership ladders later to embark on international assignments to lead and launch HR projects across the GCC, working with diverse groups from every part of the world. Each toll taught me invaluable lessons about finding and managing talents in an era we call "The War of Talent," as coined by McKinsey in 1977, aside from leadership, resilience, and emotional and social Intelligence—the tools mastered to thrive in VUCA, our modern world.

Soon after my position was made redundant, with a coaching and HR certification in hand, I moved to a Fortune 500 company that helped spark my global thinking and broadened my knowledge and expertise in the holistic and global Talent Management space, building on the Bersin by Deloitte framework. Through the ebbs and flows of the economy, VUCA, and pandemics, I witnessed waves of redundancies creating an omnipresent feeling of insecurity that pushed me to complete my MSc studies in Business Psychology with Coaching alongside my Resilience Coaching Degree, backed by deep-dive readings on emotional intelligence to help me maneuver my business and personal paths.

In reflection of the above, I came to realize that it requires wisdom to silver-line a situation, and it takes GRIT to sustain the mint. With that at the back of my mind, I started authoring, podcasting, and building my brand as a subject matter expert in the space of Leadership and Talent Management to showcase the power of properly managing talent in business. I created Nexus, my writing platform, while also writing for other esteemed global bodies. I partnered with companies, universities, and conference producers to spread further learning on smart and resilient Talent Management until I became my own brand, The Ghenwa Habbal, who is on a mission to inspire so others can aspire. A mantra I live by.

THE PROMISE OF THIS BOOK

This book is designed for HR professional, learning and development specialist, talent and business managers, leaders, and senior leaders who recognize that Emotional Intelligence (EI) is a powerful driver for organizational success. It's more than just a collection of theories and strategies; it's a testament to our shared belief in the transformative power of EI. Our experiences and insights are here to inspire you to harness the full potential of Emotional Intelligence in your professional life, just as we have in ours.

This book promises to:

- **Demystify Emotional Intelligence:** We break down the concept of Emotional Intelligence, making it both accessible and actionable so you can integrate EI seamlessly into your daily professional practice.
- **Decrypt and Identify the New Talent Management Parameters:** We crunch down traditional talent management and share the journey of its evolution and transformation in becoming a strategic business partner and a trusted sounding board at the C-suite level.
- **Explore the Intersection of Emotional Intelligence and Talent Management:** Understand how Emotional Intelligence intersects with and enhances every aspect of Talent Management, from recruitment and development to retention and succession planning, ensuring your organization thrives in the modern workplace.
- **Transform Talent Acquisition:** Discover how Emotional Intelligence can be a game-changer in talent acquisition, enabling you to select and retain individuals who are not only technically skilled but also emotionally intelligent.
- **Resolve Conflicts Constructively**: Gain strategies for using EI to navigate tensions and conflicts, turning potential disagreements into opportunities for positive outcomes and stronger relationships.

- **Elevate Leadership Effectiveness**: See how Emotional Intelligence enhances leadership by enabling leaders to connect more deeply with their teams, make sounder decisions, and lead with empathy and resilience.
- **Optimize Team Dynamics**: Understand how to leverage EI to improve team cohesion and performance, creating more effective and collaborative work environments.
- **Enhance Emotional Intelligence Through Learning and Development**: Discover how Learning and Development programs centered on EI can uplift your organization, ensuring that both leaders and employees are equipped to thrive in today's dynamic workplace.
- **Deliver Feedback with Emotional Intelligence**: In our bonus chapter, we'll show you how to give feedback with EI, turning it into a powerful tool for growth and development rather than a source of conflict or defensiveness.

This book is your guide to embedding Emotional Intelligence into key aspects of talent management, leadership, and organizational development, using the principles of the Talent Matrix to ensure not just survival but success in today's complex world.

References:

Bersin, J. (2013). The 9-Box Grid: A Framework for Talent Management. Bersin by Deloitte.

Cherniss, C. (2003). The Business Case for Emotional Intelligence. Consortium for Research on Emotional Intelligence in Organizations.

Edmondson, A. C. (1999). Psychological Safety and Learning Behavior in Work Teams. Administrative Science Quarterly, 44(2), 350-383.

Goleman, D. (1998). Working with Emotional Intelligence. Bantam Books.

*McClelland, D. C. (1999). Identifying competencies with behavioral-event interviews. *Psychological Science*, 9(5), 331-339.*

CHAPTER 1

FOUNDATION OF EMOTIONAL INTELLIGENCE

Like it or not, the corporate world is full of stories about executives who quickly climbed the ranks due to their cognitive intelligence and technical skills. Yet, many of these same leaders find themselves struggling or even failing once they reach the top. The truth is, while cognitive intelligence and technical expertise may open doors, they alone cannot prepare leaders for the complexities of sustaining success in today's fast-paced business world, where constant change is the only reality and relationships are the recipe for success.

Parallelly, the pressure at the top is massive, and it's not confined to the C-suite. It ripples through every layer of the organization, affecting everyone from executives to frontline employees. As leaders grapple with these challenges, employees must also rise to the occasion. They are tasked not only with solving complex problems and satisfying discerning customers but also with keeping up with economical, socio-political, ecological, and technological advances—all while managing immense pressure. **The gospel truth is that in such environments, it's not just about what you know but more about how you manage the unknown!**

This is where Emotional Intelligence comes into play. As stress becomes an everyday challenge, the ability to manage it effectively through EI becomes crucial. Unmanageable stress doesn't just affect individual well-being; it also undermines organizational health. When stress takes its toll, we see performance dips, productivity declines, and toxic workplace behaviors—like high turnover, backbiting, and communication breakdowns—becoming all too common. The ripple effects are significant, we know! According to the American Institute of Stress, job stress accounts for approximately one million absences each day in the U.S. alone (American Institute of Stress, 2019).

If this isn't yet a wake-up call, then what do you call it?

As leaders face these immense pressures, the traditional reliance on just Intelligence Quotient (IQ) and technical skills alone proves insufficient. Emotional Intelligence becomes the key to not just steering the ship but also weathering the storm, equipping leaders to manage these challenges with resilience and empathy. Success in this role requires more than just technical know-how or intellectual excellence; it demands adaptability, agility, managing pressures effectively, and navigating the unknown with confidence and emotional resilience. Without these qualities, even the most capable organizations can quickly descend into chaos as their workforce struggles to cope with the demands of an ever-changing environment. The COVID-19 pandemic starkly highlighted the need for emotional resilience, demonstrating that leaders who could empathize, maintain morale, and foster connection were able to guide their teams through the crisis, showing that EI is essential not just for survival but for thriving in adversity. This reality highlights a crucial insight: **it's not just about having the right tools—it's about mastering the craft of using them.**

Organizations that prioritize emotional intelligence in their talent management strategies are far better equipped to navigate these challenges. They foster a culture where employees feel valued, understood, and supported, leading to higher engagement, productivity, and retention. Research by Gallup reinforces this, showing that companies with high employee engagement outperform others by 147% in earnings per share (Gallup, 2013). Moreover, leaders with high EI can inspire and motivate their teams, create a positive work environment, and drive sustainable success, even in the face of adversity (Goleman, 1998).

So, while Intelligence Quotient (IQ) and technical skills may open doors, it's the Emotional Quotient (EQ) that determines how well individuals and organizations can truly thrive in today's volatile, uncertain, complex, and ambiguous world. This chapter will explore the foundations of Emotional Intelligence, examining its components, significance, and how it serves as a centerpiece for effective talent management.

EMOTIONAL INTELLIGENCE (EI) AS AN ENABLER

Emotional Intelligence (EI) has garnered significant attention in both psychology and business, recognized as a crucial driver of personal and professional success. Daniel Goleman, a prominent psychologist and author, defines EI as the ability to recognize, understand, and manage our own emotions, as well as the capacity to recognize, understand, and influence the emotions of others (Goleman, 1995).

At its core, Emotional Intelligence revolves around two interconnected aspects: understanding ourselves first and understanding others.

- **Knowing Yourself**: It all starts with self-awareness. This is about tuning into your emotions, understanding what triggers them, and recognizing how they influence your actions.
- **Understanding Others**: Then there's empathy. It's more than just recognizing emotions in others—it's about truly appreciating their perspectives and responding in a way that strengthens connections. This ability to see through others' eyes is what fosters trust, builds better relationships, and leads to more effective teamwork.

Interestingly, these two dimensions of Emotional Intelligence closely align with Howard Gardner's Theory of Multiple Intelligences, particularly intrapersonal intelligence (self-smart) and interpersonal intelligence (people-smart). Gardner's work expanded our understanding of intelligence, proposing that understanding oneself (intrapersonal intelligence) and understanding others (interpersonal intelligence) are as crucial as cognitive intelligence.

- **Intrapersonal Intelligence:** This is about understanding one's own emotions, strengths, and motivations. A deep sense of self-awareness empowers individuals to make informed decisions and pursue goals with confidence. In the workplace, this translates to better stress management, sound decision-making, and enhanced productivity—key drivers of career advancement (Smith & Doe, 2024; Johnson, 2023).

- **Interpersonal Intelligence:** This involves the ability to connect with others and manage relationships effectively. Empathy and understanding drive successful collaboration, leading to stronger teamwork and increased employee engagement (Brown & Green, 2022; Williams, 2021).

By linking these concepts with the broader framework of Emotional Intelligence, we can see how the ability to understand both ourselves and others forms the foundation for effective leadership and teamwork. The integration of these intelligences into the workplace is not just a theoretical exercise; it's a practical necessity for organizations that want to thrive in today's complex environment.

Figure 1.1 is based on the work of Sparrow and Maddocks (2000), and it illustrates how intrapersonal and interpersonal intelligence combine to form the core of Emotional Intelligence. This illustration highlights the crucial benefits of understanding both yourself and others, emphasizing how these intelligences intersect to strengthen Emotional Intelligence.

Figure 1.1: The Intersection of Intrapersonal and Interpersonal Intelligence in Emotional Intelligence

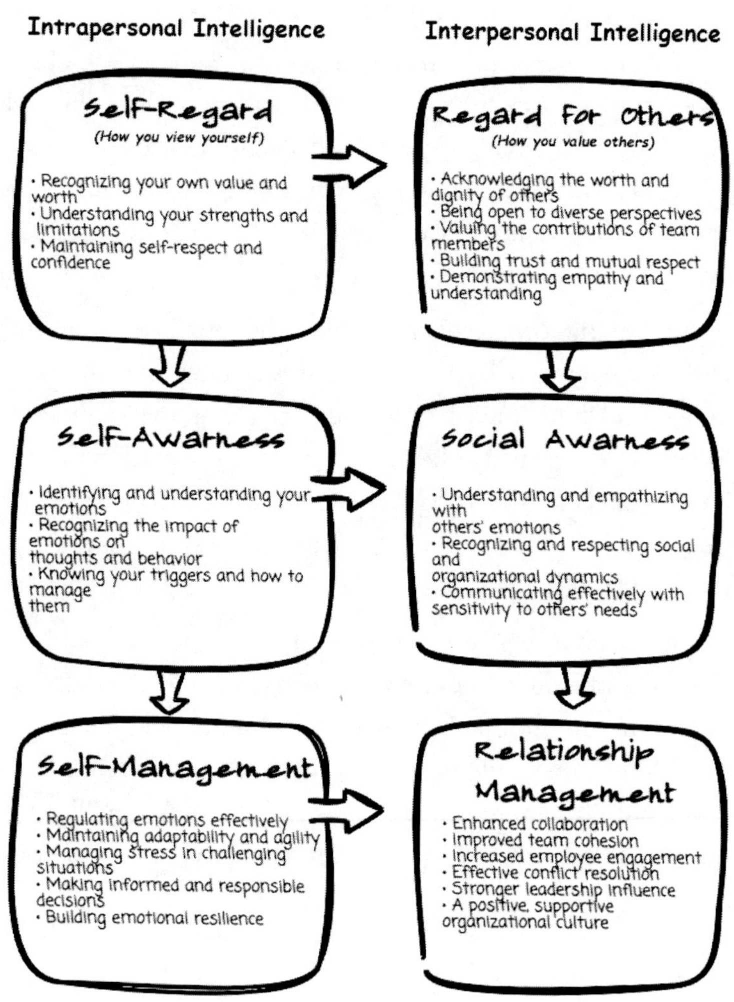

Goleman expanded on Gardner's foundational work by emphasizing that Emotional Intelligence is not just an innate trait but a skill that can be developed and enhanced. He observed that those who excel in both intrapersonal and

interpersonal intelligence are often the most successful, as they can use their emotional insights to navigate complex social interactions with empathy and finesse. This dual focus allows them to build stronger relationships, make better decisions, and create more cohesive teams.

Consider a leader navigating significant organizational change. Their self-awareness (intrapersonal intelligence) enables them to manage stress and maintain clarity in decision-making. Simultaneously, their empathy and social skills (interpersonal intelligence) empower them to communicate effectively with their team, address concerns, and foster a supportive environment. This combination of skills drives successful change management and strengthens organizational resilience.

By integrating these dimensions of intelligence, individuals can achieve a higher level of emotional and social functioning. Emotional Intelligence, therefore, is not just about surviving in a volatile, uncertain, complex, and ambiguous (VUCA) world—it's about thriving and achieving sustainable success.

But Emotional Intelligence isn't just a personal asset; it's a shared strength that influences the entire team dynamics. When even one person in a team lacks Emotional Intelligence, it can disrupt the harmony of the group, creating a ripple effect that impacts the entire organization. Our emotions and behaviors influence those around us, setting the tone for either a positive, productive environment or one filled with tension and conflict.

In contrast, employees with high Emotional Intelligence excel in areas critical to success, such as conflict management and communication. They have the ability to use their emotions as information, staying calm and objective even in high-pressure situations. For instance, picture a team racing against a tight deadline for a high-stakes project, suddenly facing an unforeseen obstacle that threatens to derail their progress. This is where leadership truly matters.

In such a scenario, a team leader with high Emotional Intelligence would be the anchor in the storm. They would quickly sense the rising stress and anxiety within the team and address it head-on. Instead of succumbing to panic or pointing fingers, this leader would stay composed, assess the situation with clarity, and encourage open communication. They might gather the team for an impromptu meeting to discuss the challenge at hand, listening empathetically to each member's concerns, validating their emotions, and reinforcing their importance to the team. By guiding a brainstorming session, the leader ensures that all ideas are heard and valued, fostering a spirit of collaboration and shared responsibility.

Contrast this with a leader who lacks Emotional Intelligence. Such a leader might react impulsively to the crisis, expressing frustration or anger, which would only heighten the tension and fear within the team. They might ignore the team's concerns, push through their own solution without discussion, or even resort to blaming others. This approach often leads to decreased morale, diminished collaboration, and ultimately lower productivity.

The takeaway? A leader with high Emotional Intelligence fosters collaboration and support, even in challenging times. Effectively managing conflicts and communicating can only strengthen team cohesion and resilience, eventually boosting performance and job satisfaction and surely increasing the chances of success.

So, what's the intrinsic nature of Emotional Intelligence? It's the ability to connect emotionally with oneself first and then with others, i.e., engaging in a deeply empathetic way, especially in the unpredictable, ever-changing times we live in. We like to call this "Emotional and Social Resonance." This resonance enables individuals to navigate the complexities of modern work environments with better fluidity, greater ease, and effectiveness. It's about creating a work culture where emotional and social connections are strong, fostering an environment of support, understanding, and shared purpose. A study published in the Journal of Organizational Behavior found that teams with high Emotional Intelligence exhibited superior problem-solving abilities and were more innovative (Jordan & Lawrence, 2009). These teams managed stress and conflict more effectively, leading to higher overall performance.

The benefits don't stop there. **Hear this out!** Research has shown that organizations with high levels of Emotional Intelligence are more resilient and adaptable. A study by Cherniss (2001) revealed that organizations investing in Emotional Intelligence training for their employees saw significant improvements in productivity and employee satisfaction. This commitment to developing Emotional Intelligence doesn't just boost individual performance—it enhances the overall effectiveness of the organization.

CAN EMOTIONAL INTELLIGENCE BE DEVELOPED?

The development of Emotional Intelligence has sparked considerable debate, but evidence increasingly supports the idea that EI is a skill that can be cultivated over time. Some believe that the Emotional Quotient (EQ), much like the Intelligence Quotient (IQ), is largely set from birth. Academically speaking and challenging that notion, a growing body of research suggests that while there may be a genetic foundation to EI, it's far from fixed. In fact, Emotional Intelligence can be developed and enhanced through life experiences and targeted training (Brackett, Rivers, & Salovey, 2011). Backed by research, it is proven that such training can lead to significant improvements in Emotional Intelligence, which ultimately boosts both personal and professional success (Cherniss, 2001).

Now, we'll discuss a tangible human-related example to enhance the imaginative, realistic visuals. Let's consider the role of age in this process. As we age, we gather a wealth of experiences that deepen our understanding of our own emotions and those of others. This maturation process can significantly boost our Emotional Intelligence (Keefer, Parker, & Saklofske, 2009), yet this does not mean growing older automatically makes us more emotionally intelligent—this is a common misconception. Instead, it's the deliberate process of reflecting on our experiences—both the highs and the lows—that fosters real growth in EI. This reflection involves understanding how our emotions influence our behavior and learning to manage them in a way that aligns with our goals.

Now, imagine that you could accelerate this development!

Targeted EI development programs, incorporating self-reflection exercises, role-playing, and ongoing feedback, can do just that—fostering genuine emotional growth that translates into improved workplace behavior and stronger relationships. These programs are designed to enhance self-awareness, improve our understanding of others' emotions, and refine our emotion management skills. But here's the crucial part—**not all development programs are created proportionately—** their effectiveness depends on targeting the right areas of the brain. Scientifically speaking, emotional processing occurs primarily in the limbic system, the 'emotional brain,' which handles memories and survival instincts but is slow to change. In contrast, the neocortex, i.e., the 'thinking brain,' excels at logic and decision-making but doesn't effectively process emotions. Effective sessions of EI training engage both systems to facilitate genuine emotional growth, incorporating both intellectual understanding and emotional practice.

Neuroscience additionally signals that developing Emotional Intelligence is not a quick fix; it's a journey. It requires consistent effort and dedication over time—think of it as a marathon, not a sprint. A brief training course or one-off workshop won't suffice. Enhancing EI is akin to embarking on a journey of personal growth. It demands a genuine commitment to self-improvement and the courage to step out of one's comfort zone.

Do you have the courage? It is a controversial question to ask yourself first and those around you as well.

As you flip the pages to our next chapter on Talent Management, remind yourself that this isn't just about checking a box or following a trend—it's about genuine transformation. Developing Emotional Intelligence is the key to building real, meaningful connections, enhancing the quality of your decisions, and enriching every aspect of your life, both personally and professionally. The road may be challenging, but the payoff is massive. In a world full of uncertainty, thriving—

not just surviving—depends on this growth. And like any true journey, the path to greater EI is a gorgonzola of continuous learning and evolution.

CHAPTER HIGHLIGHTS

- **The New Success Formula:** Emotional Intelligence is as crucial as technical skills for long-term success in today's dynamic business world.
- **Team Dynamics:** A team's performance is directly influenced by the Emotional Intelligence of its members.
- **Emotional Resilience:** Organizations with high EI are more adaptable, especially in times of crisis.
- **Brain Basics:** Effective EI development programs must engage both the emotional limbic system and the logical neocortex.
- **Continuous Growth:** Developing Emotional Intelligence is a lifelong journey that enhances relationships, decision-making, and overall well-being.

References:

Goleman, D. (1995). Emotional Intelligence: Why It Can Matter More Than IQ. Bantam Books.

American Institute of Stress. (2019). Job Stress Statistics.

Gallup. (2013). The State of the American Workplace.

*Brackett, M. A., Rivers, S. E., & Salovey, P. (2011). Emotional Intelligence: Implications for Personal, Social, Academic, and Workplace Success. *Social and Personality Psychology Compass*.*

Cherniss, C. (2001). Emotional Intelligence and Organizational Effectiveness. In C. Cherniss & D. Goleman (Eds.), The Emotionally Intelligent Workplace. Jossey-Bass.

Keefer, K. V., Parker, J. D., & Saklofske, D. H. (2009). Emotional Intelligence and Age. In J. D. Parker, D. H. Saklofske, & C. Stough (Eds.), Assessing Emotional Intelligence. Springer.

*Jordan, P. J., & Lawrence, S. A. (2009). Emotional Intelligence in Teams: Development and Initial Validation of the Short Version of the Workgroup Emotional Intelligence Profile (WEIP-S). *Journal of Organizational Behavior*.*

CHAPTER 2

DECRYPTING TALENT MANAGEMENT - REDEFINING THE PARAMETERS

Fixing it right the first time: While this is not intended to be a repair protocol nor a historical overview, it prompts an important question: How many individuals genuinely grasp the complexity and progression of talent management? To understand our current landscape, it's valuable to briefly consider how this concept has been evolving and influencing organizational practices, thus becoming more contemporary and ready for today's and tomorrow's generations.

In recent years, we have seen a significant shift in the role of talent management—from being perceived merely as a Human Resources administrative function to evolving into a crucial division dedicated to people and business growth. Talent Management in organizations today is increasingly focusing on building "Future of Work" ready hubs through cultivating a workforce that strategically contributes to profitability rather than simply filling vacancies. To better illustrate this point, we invite you to envision the wider organization as an orchestra.

Each department within an organization plays its own unique instrument—operations oversee sales and performance; marketing and communications strategize for employer and corporate branding, while leadership shapes strategic direction. However, without someone orchestrating these efforts from a human perspective—a conductor—the resulting symphony fails to resonate harmoniously. Talent management serves as that essential conductor, ensuring all parts of the organization collaborate effectively toward shared success through culture and beyond practices like how finance oversees the financial fitness of the organization.

Despite these advancements, discussions surrounding talent management remain incomplete; there is still much work needed regarding how it tackles the wicked challenges presented by today's modern—diverse, dynamic, and demanding—workforce. In this chapter, we aim to explore these contemporary concepts, leveraging our combined extensive research and experience gained from working at and alongside multinational firms. This allows us to analyze global internal talent administration insightfully, thus providing you with rich context across various settings that are also influenced by various research-based frameworks, such as those described in Bersin by Deloitte's Talent Management model (Bersin 2013).

DECRYPTING THE TERM "TALENT MANAGEMENT"

Crunching down talent management is only fair and rational today, as it is far more than just a buzzword. I'm just saying it's a strategic imperative at the core of an organization's success.

At its essence, talent management goes beyond attracting and retaining employees; it is the whole nine yards in between. In other words, it's about nurturing, developing, and optimizing individuals with the skills and potential to meet both current and future organizational demands (Cappelli, 2008). Thinking otherwise surely defies the efforts of talent management professionals and enthusiasts about the continuous commitments they have towards fostering inspiring workplaces focused on creating inclusive, fair, and psychologically safe environments that entail robust career growth processes built on progressive performance management programs.

Ultimately, brilliant talent management professionals are positive and sure about one thing: for their talents to thrive, they should aim to create exceptional workplace experiences, train their people to navigate cultural diversity with empathy and insight, and help embrace technological advancements aligned with their organization's strategic goals and objectives (Collings & Mellahi, 2009). Yet the exponential question is, "How can we arrive at common ground with the other C-Suite members 10x faster, considering knowledge, disruption, and scalability barriers?"

UNDERSTANDING CONTEMPORARY TALENT MANAGEMENT

We do not fear the word Revolution! Rather, our concern lies in the world's inability to embrace vulnerability and recognize the necessity for adaptation in this era of contemporary brilliance. This new age demands swift adjustments and innovative strategies, and those who fail to keep pace risk being left behind.

As we nudge ourselves, too, we remind you once again that today's talent management scenery has evolved beyond the pure transactional HR role; it has transformed into a dynamic, data-driven vigor that emphasizes precision, inclusivity, agility, and a relentless dedication to innovation. Organizations are no longer passively managing talent; they are radically changing how they attract, develop, and retain high-caliber individuals while cultivating an empathetic and inclusive work environment.

Seeing the future in more expansive ways requires you to envision a larger, comprehensive talent management approach—an omnichannel system that seamlessly integrates various platforms to oversee the employee lifecycle. This strategy requires you to question and investigate the unknown first and unfold trends through experience and imaginative curiosity. Thus, it ensures a consistent experience across talent acquisition, mobility, onboarding, performance evaluations, learning and development, as well as career progression. Furthermore, by implementing continuous feedback loops and leveraging data-driven insights, we believe organizations can make real-time adjustments to their talent strategies. All tried and tested. Without a doubt, this alignment to business objectives enhances the holistic employee ecosystem, as it should be followed by continuous and consistent personalized communication and strategic marketing efforts.

Furthermore, understanding contemporary talent management, we shed light on the emergence of the gig economy—this phenomenon represents a significant transformative shift in work and is surely not a fleeting trend.

So, as organizations strive to balance the interests of full-time employees with those of gig workers, there is an increasing reliance on talent management professionals. These experts are required to spearhead efforts in upskilling and reskilling across diverse avenues to navigate the competitive landscape for talent successfully. For instance, we find talent management professionals today collaborating with other functions in the business to establish talent marketplaces, alongside forming agile teams to work on projects across the organization, which can enhance employees' knowledge and experience while simultaneously developing a strong pipeline of future leaders for effective succession planning amidst uncertainty.

Not to forget, investing in simple and bold innovative learning and development strategies while also leveraging the power of artificial intelligence-based learning, such as byte-size personalized learning, has become essential given the speed of things and humans' short attention spans. Such an approach lays the foundation for an organizational culture that prioritizes ongoing growth and ingenuity.

In summary, contemporary talent management is shifting away from traditional economies of scale toward what is termed **'economies of learning,'** a term that caught our attention during our research rounds on how to master the development of business strategies for success inspired by Besanko et al., who discuss the "economic theory." This non-magical force marks out the benefits derived from continuous improvement, innovation, and knowledge acquisition—leveraging expertise from across the board to enhance efficiency and resilience as well as regeneration in an unpredictable world is the only given.

The key takeaway? If talent management teams can master these aspects, they will be well-prepared to navigate the dilemma of a VUCA environment—the future favors those who not only anticipate change but actively reshape it as pioneers.

REDEFINING THE PARAMETERS OF CONTEMPORARY TALENT MANAGEMENT

To envision the future with greater breadth, one must be open to delving into the unfamiliar expansive inquiry and learning we shared earlier. This involves analyzing evolving trends from various perspectives and experiences, which enhances our capacity to recognize interconnected systems and their broader consequences. It also calls for a willingness to nurture our curiosity, imagination, and capacity for dreaming, no matter how farfetched it can get.

This process requires diligent observation of macro forces such as environmental shifts, technological advancements, and demographic transformations that will significantly alter our world. Forward-thinking individuals do not simply react to current crises; they seek out deeper patterns and underlying dynamics. They are open to setting aside immediate concerns regarding feasibility or financial practicality in pursuit of bold visions powered by imaginative application. Again, it was the missing toilet paper that shocked and shook the world! So, if talent management leaders consider one thing they could do differently to help the organizations and people they serve be future-ready, where would they start?

With a sustainable, emotionally intelligent, resilient lens, we say!

In 2024, the Talent Management role, as a divisional business partner, is more crucial than ever in navigating the uncertain world. The stakes are high, and companies are demanding tact, speed, and agility in purposefully filling and elevating their talent pipelines, as well as implementing human-centered performance enhancement and succession planning programs that deliver quick, tangible returns and have their people upskilled and ready to offer solutions to the world rather than creating them. Accordingly, this is believed to be net positive. It is all about humanity and how much you care today. Ultimately, we say that the condo of humanity, humility, and the larger mission of oneself combined eventually provide strength to people and organizations when the Richter Scale 9 earthquake hits.

In this post-modern era—a time characterized by a relentless challenge to cultural and intellectual norms—and as Talent Management becomes increasingly inevitable, executives are further demanding that talent professionals develop robust plans addressing sustainable ESG (Environmental, Social, and Governance) and JEDIBA (Just, Equitable, Diverse, Inclusive, Belonging, and Accessible) metrics. They want solutions that strike the perfect balance, addressing what matters most to the business, its people, and the consumers simultaneously, with a vision that considers both the long-term horizon and immediate needs. So, let's be honest—2024 onward is the year where the proof will be in the revamped talent pudding endorsed by the parameters below.

Parameter 1: The Impact of Technology

Let's face it: technology is where the revolution begins. The digital age has ushered in a wave of technological interventions that have transformed the human resources field, making processes faster, smarter, and more efficient with just a click. For instance, finding the right talent has always been a challenge, but as technology continues to evolve, talent management teams can now hire and customize communication with unprecedented speed and precision. They can analyze vast amounts of data, uncover underlying patterns, and make more informed decisions that resonate with leadership. This is not just about being efficient; it's about being strategic and proactive in a way that was unimaginable just a few years ago. Let's think of Virtual Reality and Metaverse experience when hiring!

Parameter 2: Global Workforce Trends

While technology is a fundamental parameter, it is only part of the equation. The globalization of the workforce is another primary driver reshaping how organizations operate. In today's interconnected world, the marketplace knows no borders. Aspiring for a niche skill set just became handy! This has led teams to become more culturally diverse and geographically dispersed than ever, bringing a wealth of perspectives and ideas that can drive innovation beyond expectations.

However, we know that managing a globally dispersed team does not come without challenges. Geographical leadership and management require a nuanced understanding of cultural diversity and a tireless commitment to inclusivity. Additionally, it is key to remind ourselves of the legal and regulatory complexities that come with a global workforce. As companies expand their reach, they must navigate an increasingly complex web of regulations that can vary dramatically from one region to another. This complexity is amplified by the rise of the gig economy—a trend we touched on earlier. The gig economy isn't just a blip on the radar; it's a seismic shift that's changing the way we think about employment, too. More and more professionals are turning to gig work for the flexibility and autonomy it offers, forcing organizations to rethink traditional employment models. The challenge, of course, sits with finding ways to effectively manage gig workers alongside full-time employees, creating a cohesive and productive workforce despite the differences in employment types.

Parameter 3: Changing Employee Expectations

If the workforce is evolving, so are the expectations of employees. Today's workforce—shaped by millennials, Generation Z, and soon, Generation Alpha—has a very different set of priorities compared to the previous generations. Gone are the days when job security and a steady paycheck were the primary motivators. Instead, employees now seek work-life balance, meaningful and purposeful work, and ample opportunities for growth and social exposure. These are not just perks, but they're non-negotiables for a generation that values freedom, purpose, and personal development above all else.

Now, employers must stand out in a crowded marketplace by offering more than just competitive salaries. They need to align with the values of their prospective employees, particularly those in the younger generations who crave exquisite work experience, ongoing learning, and both personal and professional growth; otherwise, the gig economy is just next door. Therefore, organizations today are bound to implement flexible work arrangements, thus offering remote work options and flexible hours, which have ultimately attracted top talent back from their gig life to a certain extent, as well as witnessed a significant boost in their innovative processes and employee satisfaction and retention rates.

Call it fair greed! Today's employees also expect a level of personalization in their work experience that previous generations never dreamed of. They want benefits that are tailored to their individual needs, health, and insurance plans, given the rise of stress levels, and they seek career paths that are customized to fit their unique goals. Flexible work arrangements, such as remote work and adaptable hours, are no longer just nice-to-haves; they are expectations. The pandemic proved something powerful, i.e., productivity and collaboration don't have to happen within the confines of a physical office. As a result, a significant portion of the workforce now expects the option to work remotely, or at least part-time.

This brings us to a critical realization about the current "wicked" state of talent management. We're navigating a disrupted landscape reshaped by emotional intelligence, empowered by technology, and influenced by the complexities of global workforce management. But at the heart of it all are the employees—the lifeblood of any organization—whose new demands and expectations are redefining what it means to manage talent in the twenty-first century.

As a result, organizations that embrace this shift and adapt to these changing expectations will not only establish best-in-class practices but will also become the employers of choice for the next generation. Success in the modern workplace requires thinking ahead. Leveraging data to make informed decisions, investing in learning and development, and fostering deep employee engagement to retain top talent has always been tough, but it's not an impossible task only if you're willing to do it right.

ALL ABOUT THE QUANTUM LEAP

Last but certainly not least: Talent leaders today are so much more than gatekeepers of resumes or enforcers of HR policies.

They are visionaries, strategists, therapists to a certain extent, and above all, creators. Like entrepreneurs, they are constantly innovating and adapting, always on the hunt for opportunities to cultivate and harness the potential within their direct and wider organization's teams, understanding that this requires a dual mindset of a "consultant" and an "entrepreneur," where agility, creativity, and a deep understanding of human behavior are paramount.

Therefore, we advocate…

Great Talent Management Professionals think like entrepreneurs and creators first and Human Resources Professionals second. This idea isn't just inspired by the brilliance of thought leaders like Patty McCord, who helped reinvent HR at Netflix, but it's a call to action for all talent leaders. It's about embracing a new identity, one that goes beyond the conventional HR playbook and instead prioritizes innovation and strategic foresight.

NOW is the time for Chief Talent Management Officers (CTMOs) to step up and take the quantum leap that Chief Financial Officers (CFOs) did in the past when they became the indispensable voice in the CEO's mind. It's time for the G3—an elite force group comprising the Chief Executive Officer (CEO), Chief Financial Officer (CFO), and Chief Talent Management Officer (CTMO)—to join forces with the rest of the executive team to manage human capital and unlock the organization's true potential.

For these extraordinary elite forces to rock the world, Chief Talent Management Officers must master the power of Emotional Intelligence.

These shifts have redefined what it means to be "talented." No longer is talent just a bundle of current skills and past experiences; it's about potential—the ability to grow, adapt, and thrive in today's environments and tomorrow's world. This is where the true power of talent management lies, and this is the quantum leap that CTMOs must embrace to lead meaningful change within their organizations.

To truly understand the quantum leap required in talent management, it's essential to compare the old ways with the new. F**igure 2.1,** i.e., Key Distinctive Behaviors Between Conventional and Contemporary Talent Management, below outlines the key differences between conventional, armored approaches and contemporary, daring strategies that drive intrapreneurship and set the stage for quantum transformation.

Figure 2.1: Key Distinctive Behaviors Between

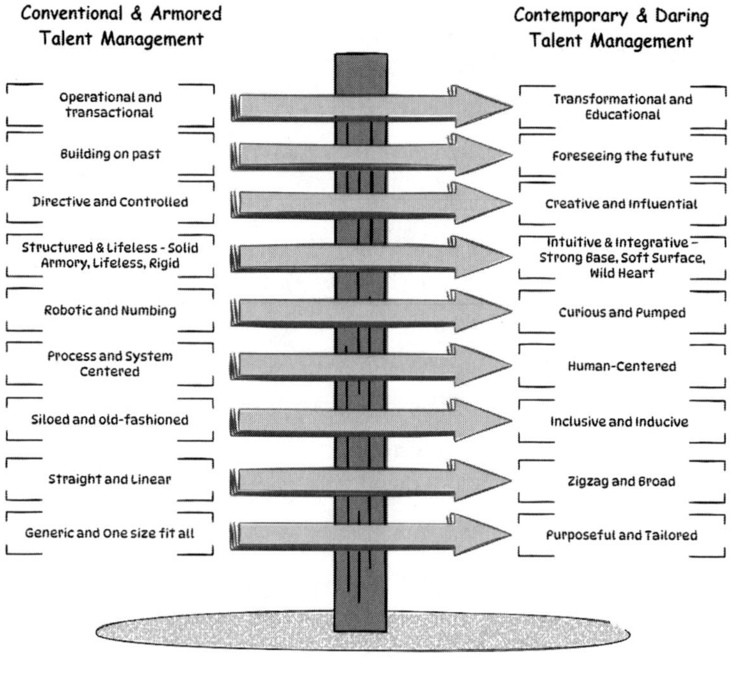

Conventional and Contemporary Talent Management

CLOSING THOUGHTS

Getting real moment: Reinventing talent management isn't just about adopting new digital technologies or rolling out fresh policies. It's about cultivating a mindset that celebrates change, diversity, and continuous improvement, all through the lens of Emotional Intelligence and beyond. Organizations that get this right will not only attract and retain the best talent but will also position themselves as leaders in innovation and competitiveness within their industries. Maintaining a connection to the present while simultaneously investing deeply in future possibilities creates a formidable strategy, just like automotive companies who are fully committing to the future of electric vehicles while still producing combustion engines for the time being, and who knows when they might also transition to solar?

In summary, on reinventing talent management, we urge you to consistently debate the 30 years of utopia and dystopia in emerging talent management because talent management done right makes a stride.

CHAPTER HIGHLIGHTS

- **Talent Management Evolution:** Talent management is now a central strategic process focused on nurturing and optimizing individuals for current and future needs.
- **Contemporary Challenges:** Globalization, technology, and changing workforce demographics demand agile, innovative, and forward-thinking talent management.
- **Technological Impact:** AI and big data have transformed talent management, enabling strategic, efficient, and informed decision-making.
- **Global Workforce and Gig Economy:** Managing a diverse, global workforce and the rise of gig work requires understanding cultural diversity and regulatory complexities.
- **Employee Expectations:** Attracting top talent now requires aligning with values like work-life balance, meaningful work, and flexible arrangements.
- **Emotional Intelligence and Innovation:** Modern talent management demands a mindset embracing change, diversity, and continuous improvement through Emotional Intelligence.
- **CTMOs' Role:** Chief Talent Management Officers must lead with Emotional Intelligence to drive strategic initiatives and unlock organizational potential.

References:

Bersin, J. (2013). Predictions for 2013: Corporate Talent, Leadership, and HR—Nexus of Global Forces Drives New Models for Talent. Bersin by Deloitte.

Cappelli, P. (2008). Talent on Demand: Managing Talent in an Age of Uncertainty. Harvard Business Press.

*Collings, D. G., & Mellahi, K. (2009). Strategic talent management: A review and research agenda. *Human Resource Management Review*, 19(4), 304-313.*

McKinsey & Company. (1997). The War for Talent. McKinsey Quarterly.

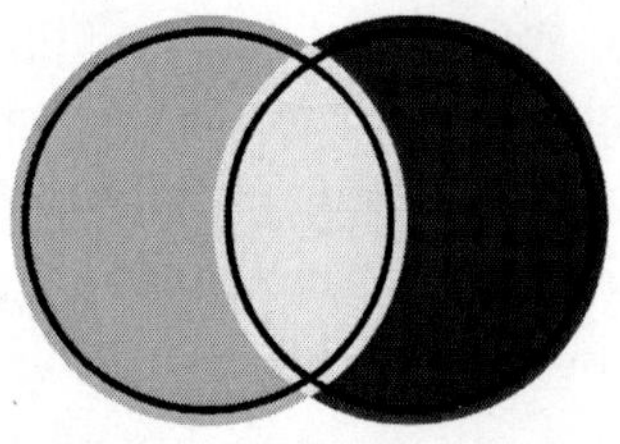

CHAPTER 3

THE INTERSECTION BETWEEN EMOTIONAL INTELLIGENCE AND TALENT MANAGEMENT

In today's relentless quest and as businesses continue to search hopelessly for the elusive edge, many organizations find conventional management disciplines are inadequate for confronting the disorienting climate that always pervades this period. That, in practice, requires more sophisticated ways to manage people, and one approach that is aggressively gaining traction is the incorporation of Emotional Intelligence (EI) into Talent Management, previously called "human resources" activities. EQ, for example, or the capacity for recognizing, understanding, and controlling one's emotions, in addition to others, too, has become a vital skill in nurturing a flexible, capable labor force that can keep up with change.

Ready or not, the future of lucid Talent Management hinges on Emotional Intelligence. This bold concept, we know, is now not just an opinion but a fact. It is a deep understanding of emotions that determines how well we manage our energy, how well we get along with others, and even our state of mind. In other words, emotional competencies have a deep impact on leadership effectiveness, team dynamics, workplace productivity, and the overall organizational culture. What Emotional Intelligence brings to individuals and their organizations, as laid out in earlier parts of this book, are fundamental changes in habits and attitudes. When it is done in conjunction with modern Talent Management practices, it ultimately transforms traditional offerings to become more versatile and strategically necessary for today's rambling business environments.

In chapter 1, we set a foundation with the basics of Emotional Intelligence: what it involves and how the concept can be transformative in both work and private life. We also looked later at what is happening at present as Talent Management goes beyond conventional practices to incorporate broader, more coordinated strategies essential for surviving today's unpredictable business terrain.

Relying on the principle of Emotional Intelligence, traced back in earlier chapters, through its fundamental building blocks of self-awareness and empathy, this chapter examines how these principles can be used strategically in Talent Management. Therefore, if and when these principles are applied within an organization, it can manage the complexities of today's world better and ensure both personal and corporate development.

UNDERSTANDING THE SYNERGY EFFECT

We all have experienced a rocked world by multifaceted challenges that have converged to disrupt the beliefs, health, well-being, and economies of humans. For sure, no one has escaped. Thus, a shared experience of speculations and possibilities leads to new ways of thinking that reveal themselves in the actions, words, and behaviors of companies, leaders, and systems, trickling down to daily lives and causing uncertainty. This vicious push-and-pull mechanism hits organizations and human confidence, which, in turn, hits creativity, productivity, performance, loyalty, and profitability—the full-on livelihood of the greater world symphony.

Yet, the giant mutation of Emotional Intelligence merging with Talent Management in organizations is nothing short of what we call "metamorphosis." A transformation that reshapes the essence of human and organizational leadership and evolution. This process enriches interpersonal dynamics within the workplace, fostering a culture of resilience, adaptability, and a profound human-centered approach. In humble words, this fusion makes communication among coworkers more fun and humane so that the office and the overall work environment remain congenial and collegial.

So, How Does Emotional Intelligence Reshape Talent and Performance?

Leveraging the "Talent Matrix," also the title of the book you are reading that incorporates binary numbers in its design, is pivotal in identifying and managing talent based on performance and potential. As you may know, it helps categorize employees in a way that highlights both high performers and high potential, guiding developmental and strategic placement decisions within any organization. The strategic approach of this matrix avoids binary thinking by recognizing a spectrum of employee attributes and contributions, encouraging a non-binary understanding that values diverse skill sets, competencies, and growth trajectories. This approach is particularly important in a VUCA world, where rigid categories fail to capture the nuanced realities of employee performance.

As we now bridge this to the matrix of Emotional Intelligence, we find that such matrix reshapes talent and performance by providing a strategic guide for applying emotional intelligence across diverse talent management functions. This synergy is reflected in the actions outlined in **Table 3.1,** which illustrates how Emotional Intelligence can transform key areas of talent management—from talent acquisition to conflict resolution—into a harmonious ecosystem that promotes growth, collaboration, and resilience.

Table 3.1: The Giant Mutation Driven by Emotional Intelligence

Arena	When Intersecting with Emotional Intelligence can...
Talent Acquisition and Mobility	**It determines the stability and appeal of a solid skyscraper.** Traditional hiring practices often prioritize technical skills, but we need to acknowledge that while technical proficiency opens the door, it's emotional intelligence that drives long-term success. Shifting our focus when hiring or rotating candidates on those who demonstrate high emotional intelligence through tested scenario-based assessments, along with other intelligence quotients, helps co-create a positive and resilient work environment. Humans with high EQ can manage to stress better, triumph in collaboration across diverse teams, and inspire innovative solutions.

Talent Orientation and Onboarding	**It accelerates the lucid state of performance.** Embedding EI behaviors during the new hires' journey, despite the role and candidate seniority, connects them with the company's culture and values, speeds up their integration, and boosts their confidence and effectiveness from the outset, aiding engagement and commitment at speed. This process goes beyond simple job training, facilitating the building of meaningful relationships across functions and teams that anchor new employees more firmly within the organization. It is about building trust, lowering anxiety, building rapport faster, and offering a feeling of being welcomed.
Performance Management and Succession Planning	**It doubles down on radical performance and profitability.** Constructing an emotional intelligence lens during performance check-ins shifts the belief that it is no longer a penalty and punishment session but rather a strategic touchpoint to evaluate what went well through understanding the "how" and "what" via open dialogue based on facts and honest discussions about strength for the future and career aspirations. Furthermore, it is a great connecting point, allowing remarkable recognition for the good work done and realignment on the next steps. It is all about employee satisfaction, the greatest asset of all time and the most expensive in the books of the CFOs, yet the most needed in the lives of CTMOs and CEOs.

Learning and Leadership Professional Development	**It serves as the oracle of transforming people and programs.** Capitalizing on emotional intelligence centered programs and strategies is the instrument that transforms the stakeholders learning and development professional experiences. Emotional intelligence can help leaders better respond to their people's emotions, aspirations, and performance check-in discussions. Furthermore, it helps learning professionals understand the psychology of their working society, enabling tailored and customized learning interventions and paths building on the people's areas of excellence and growth opportunities while bringing the power of artificial intelligence to center stage. As a matter of fact, emotional intelligence promotes empathy, resilience, and adaptability, helping employees across the board to cope with wicked daily challenges and help them steer the change in their own learning journeys to higher their levels of self-awareness and performance delivery.
Conflict Resolutions and Management	**It navigates disputes with empathy, understanding, and better communication.** A workforce with high emotional intelligence can recognize and manage their emotions and those of others, thus de-escalating tensions and fostering a calm, constructive atmosphere for resolving conflicts. It facilitates active listening, which is crucial for landing mutually accepted solutions. Furthermore, it equips people with the skill of approaching conflicts with an open mindset, thus reducing defensiveness and rather focusing on finding a solution to the problem at hand. Eventually, an emotionally intelligent community is considered a positively charged society where people value relationships built on the foundation of respect and trust above all.

As we scale up some of the research we conducted, we summarize and share...

In a study conducted by the Consortium for Research on Emotional Intelligence in Organizations at L'Oreal, some eye-opening results were revealed. Sales agents selected based on their emotional competence generated an additional $91,370 per year compared to their counterparts, leading to a net revenue increase of over $2.5 million annually (Cherniss, 2003). This isn't just a statistic; it's a powerful demonstration of how Emotional Intelligence can directly enhance sales performance and profitability.

Additionally, at a global Fortune 500 company, research found that divisions with higher emotional intelligence scores reported 34% higher profit growth compared to those with lower EI scores. This isn't just about individual performance; this is about driving broader organizational success (McClelland, 1999). The correlation is clear: cultivating emotionally intelligent teams isn't just beneficial for employee morale; it's a strategic advantage that impacts the bottom line.

Here's where things get exciting. A real-life manufacturing plant decided to take a leap and invest in emotional intelligence training. And the results? Pretty astonishing. Lost-time accidents dropped from 50 a year to just 5. And if that's not impressive enough, formal grievances plummeted by 80%. It's a powerful example of how fostering emotional intelligence isn't just about creating a 'feel-good' atmosphere—it's about real, tangible changes that make the workplace safer, smoother, and more collaborative (Cherniss, 2003). These numbers speak for themselves, showing just how much EI can transform an organization.

In a nutshell, adopting emotional intelligence principles first and then adapting to them creates a more inclusive and motivating work environment where employees feel engaged, valued, and understood, leading to higher retention and satisfaction.

Have you connected the dots now? We're not just talking about a marginal improvement; we're talking about that quantum leap you experienced earlier in previous chapters on how organizations operate. It is the strategic infusion of emotional intelligence into your talent management practices. It is the chemical combustion that happens in labs that you're overlooking.

CORE COMPETENCIES AT THE INTERSECTION

At the heart of the intersection between Emotional Intelligence and Talent Management discussed earlier lies a set of core competencies that are pivotal for transformative and sustainable success. These competencies are the building blocks that enhance the 360-degree views of Talent Management from a humanistic perspective now.

Empathy It is more than just understanding others; it's about creating deeper connections within teams and across the organization. In managing talent, empathy enables the development of more inclusive and supportive workplace policies and practices, crucial during times of organizational restructuring, for example. Maintaining morale and ensuring the well-being of those impacted empathetically becomes a key driver of a resilient workforce.	**Self-awareness** It is just another cornerstone competency. It's central to both personal development and effective management. A self-aware leader recognizes their biases and limitations, leading to more equitable and informed decision-making. This competency also aligns career paths with individuals' genuine strengths and aspirations, ensuring that personal fulfillment is in sync with organizational goals. Self-awareness is the foundation of authentic leadership and meaningful talent development.
Motivation It is the engine that drives engagement and retention strategies. Understanding what truly motivates individuals within your organization allows for the creation of tailored behaviors and programs that resonate with their aspirations and ambitions. This approach doesn't just enhance job satisfaction; it significantly boosts overall productivity and fuels a culture of continuous growth and achievement.	**Leadership** Leadership infused with emotional intelligence transcends the outdated command-and-control model of the past. We like to say, **Go Big or Go Home!** Emotional intelligence-driven leadership practices build trust, encourage open communication, and cultivate a positive organizational climate. This approach is especially critical for managing diverse teams and sustaining high performance, even in challenging circumstances.

We draw our inspiration from these multifaceted competencies because we've seen firsthand how they can be a remedy for many of the challenges organizations face today. Our belief is rooted not just in theory but in practice—years of coaching and working within global organizations and professionals have shown us that when Emotional Intelligence is integrated with Talent Management practices, it transforms the psychological well-being of both systems and individuals. The result is a more forward-thinking and responsive environment, capable of not just meeting challenges but thriving in the ever-evolving ecosystem.

EMOTIONAL INTELLIGENCE AS A STRATEGIC TALENT MANAGEMENT TOOL

Let's think radically for a moment. Imagine Emotional Intelligence as the differentiator circuit in electronics—a critical component that enhances signal processing. In the context of Talent Management, EI serves a similar role, enriching the quality of your talent management deliverables through strengthened interactions and relationships within your organization's culture.

Here's the million-dollar question: "How do you foster Emotional Intelligence at both personal and organizational levels simultaneously?"

When we first delved into the intersection of Emotional Intelligence and Talent Management, we knew that simply sharing our insights with teams and communities wasn't enough. We needed to dig deeper to understand the barriers that prevent the integration of EI into Talent Management practices.

Looking back, while emotional intelligence is not new, in its simplest form, it is regulating emotions that eventually reshape and elevate talent and performance. To back up our findings about the value of Emotional Intelligence we looked at popular research in the field, including Simon Sinek's "Start with Why," Adam Grant's "Givers and Takers," and Marshall Goldsmith's "Triggers," aside from the plethora of research available on Harvard Business Review, which granted us a solid foundation of the value and importance of Emotional Intelligence as a critical component of success.

Leveraging the experience and expertise we've gathered, we reached the assumption that the complex surrounding **e**nvironment, compounded by fast-paced technological advancement, makes people more **r**esistant to change, leading to a growing **i**gnorance of the surrounding **s**ituations over time. To help shift this narrative, we introduce RISE—a framework we developed to tackle these challenges head-on. As outlined in **Table 3.2,** the RISE framework offers a practical way to identify and overcome barriers to Emotional Intelligence, encouraging reflection and setting actionable SMART goals.

Table 3.2: Overcoming Barriers to Emotional Intelligence in Talent Management

ACRONYM	MEANING	QUESTIONS TO ASK YOURSELF	SMART GOALS YOU SET FOR YOURSELF
R	Resistance	List the things that make you resistant to change.	
I	Ignorance	List the things or behaviors you exercised that led you to become ignorant.	

S	Surrounding Situation	List some of the tools at hand you dropped that hindered your success in tackling a situation.	
E	Environment	List biases that did not aid your quest or search to find the differentiator.	

As a result, we firmly believe that when we recognize the significance of Emotional Intelligence and actively promote its development among employees, leaders, and organizations, we can cultivate a culture infused with psychological safety. In other words, businesses and business professionals have become miles away from the so-called naive organizations or humans.

EMOTIONAL INTELLIGENCE AS A BUSINESS IMPERATIVE

Here's a thought: What if Emotional Intelligence isn't just a nice-to-have but the very backbone of effective leadership and culture? Think about it—if a team doesn't trust each other, if leaders aren't truly in tune with their people, can any real progress happen? EI doesn't just boost skills; it fuels the kind of leadership that turns a workplace into a thriving, resilient space where people want to give their best.

So, how does this all play out in the real world? Emotional Intelligence isn't just about 'feeling good' at work; it's the catalyst that drives effective leadership and a strong organizational culture. Let's break down exactly how EI magnifies these critical elements and why it's so impactful.

Leadership Effectiveness and Organizational Culture: When Emotional Intelligence becomes part of the culture, its impact on leadership effectiveness and organizational synergy is magnified exponentially. Think of emotional intelligence as analogous to a differentiator circuit in electronics. It has the unique ability to amplify and highlight the most crucial elements of organizational culture. Individuals with high emotional intelligence excel in comprehending and regulating their own emotions, especially during stressful times, and are equally adept at understanding the emotions of others. This mastery fosters enhanced communication, collaboration, and overall team synergy, all of which are vital in creating a workplace that prioritizes well-being.

Emotional Intelligence is key to building a psychologically safe environment—one where trust, respect, and open communication are the norm. As Amy Edmondson (1999) highlighted, this kind of environment is essential for fostering innovation and collaboration. When organizations invest in developing high EI among employees, they create a culture where creativity and performance can truly thrive.

When employees demonstrate elevated Emotional Intelligence, they are not just navigating their own emotional landscapes; they are also nurturing a workplace atmosphere characterized by trust, respect, and psychological safety. This, in turn, stimulates creativity, innovation, and superior performance. By acknowledging and valuing the emotions and perspectives of others, emotionally intelligent individuals play a pivotal role in establishing a more inclusive and harmonious workplace.

Ultimately, it's this blend of Emotional Intelligence and psychological safety that transforms organizational culture into a dynamic, resilient, and thriving ecosystem, one where employees are empowered to perform at their best, collaborate freely, and contribute to the organization's long-term success.

Navigating Change and Transformation for Organization Excellence: This journey doesn't stop there. Emotional Intelligence continues to operate as a distinctive force within organizational cultures, setting apart individuals who can adeptly navigate intricate interpersonal dynamics with both finesse and empathy. In today's diverse and fast-paced work settings, the ability to effectively understand and respond to the emotions of colleagues, clients, and stakeholders is critical to achieving success. Leaders with high Emotional Intelligence don't just manage, but they inspire. They resolve conflicts with empathy, create psychologically safe environments, and build robust relationships founded on mutual trust and understanding.

In the end, the journey to organizational excellence—one that spans a thousand miles—begins with the commitment to cultivate an emotionally intelligent organization. Through all its ebbs and flows, this commitment is the foundation of long-term success, as illustrated in **Figure 3.3** below.

Figure 3.3: Contributing essential elements to organizational excellence

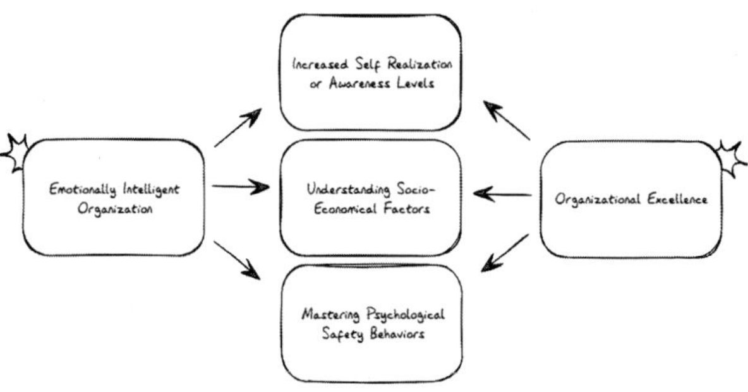

FINAL THOUGHTS

Here's the bottom line: Emotional Intelligence isn't just a "nice to have" in talent management; it's the game-changer. When you combine the principles of EI with modern talent management strategies, you're not just managing people, but you're transforming your workforce into a more adaptable, resilient, and high-performing team. It's about understanding that your people are more than just skill sets. They're human beings with emotions, aspirations, and unique contributions.

By integrating Emotional Intelligence into talent acquisition, onboarding, performance management, and leadership development, you elevate your organization from merely functioning to thriving. The result? A culture that not only survives but thrives in today's unpredictable, fast-paced world. And the data backs it up—from enhanced productivity and creativity to increased profitability.

So, what's the challenge? It's committing to the journey. By fostering a culture where Emotional Intelligence isn't just a buzzword but a core value, you're setting your organization up for long-term success. Remember, the future of talent management doesn't lie in rigid processes—it's found at the intersection of human connection and strategic insight. And that's where the magic really happens.

CHAPTER HIGHLIGHTS

- **Strategic Role of EI in Talent Management:** Emotional Intelligence (EI) is crucial for modern Talent Management, enhancing leadership, team dynamics, and organizational culture.
- **Key EI Competencies:** Empathy, self-awareness, motivation, and leadership are pivotal in driving successful Talent Management.
- **Research-Backed Benefits:** EI integration leads to significant improvements in sales, profitability, safety, and employee relations.
- **Overcoming Barriers:** The RISE framework (Resistance, Ignorance, Surrounding Situations, Environment) helps address obstacles to EI implementation.
- **EI's Cultural Impact:** EI fosters psychological safety and a positive organizational culture, driving innovation and performance.
- **Leadership and Transformation:** EI empowers leaders to navigate change and build a resilient, high-performing organization.

References:

Cherniss, C. (2003). The Business Case for Emotional Intelligence. Consortium for Research on Emotional Intelligence in Organizations. Retrieved from http://www.eiconsortium.org/reports/business_case_for_ei.html

Edmondson, A. C. (1999). Psychological safety and learning behavior in work teams. Administrative Science Quarterly, 44(2), 350-383.

Goleman, D. (1995). Emotional Intelligence: Why It Can Matter More Than IQ. Bantam Books.

McClelland, D. C. (1999). Identifying competencies with behavioral-event interviews. Psychological Science, 9(5), 331-339.

Sinek, S. (2009). Start with Why: How Great Leaders Inspire Everyone to Take Action. Portfolio.

Grant, A. (2013). Give and Take: A Revolutionary Approach to Success. Penguin Books.

Goldsmith, M. (2015). Triggers: Creating Behavior That Lasts—Becoming the Person You Want to Be. Crown Business.

CHAPTER 4

EMOTIONAL INTELLIGENCE AND TALENT ACQUISITION

AT THIS POINT, we all understand the importance of Emotional intelligence. But here's the real question: How often do we bring that into Talent Acquisition, a space where technical skills usually steal the spotlight? Let's be honest: When was the last time you heard someone say, "We hired them because they have incredible empathy, self-awareness, and adaptability?" Probably not too often, right? But here's the kicker: those qualities are game-changers in the workplace.

Research proves it: employees with high Emotional Intelligence don't just excel at managing themselves—they create thriving environments that fuel organizational growth (Cherniss, 2003). And yet, in recruitment, we tend to focus more on qualifications, experience, and technical expertise, completely overlooking the emotional and interpersonal skills that actually elevate a team.

You've made the perfect hire on paper—strong qualifications, excellent track record, technical know-how—but something still doesn't click. Why? It might be because we often overlook Emotional Intelligence when it matters the most. Let's take a step back and look at how EI impacts not just candidates but recruiters themselves.

REFLECTING ON RECRUITERS' EMOTIONAL INTELLIGENCE

Let's flip the script for a second. When was the last time you, as a recruiter, took stock of your own emotional intelligence? Sure, we focus on evaluating candidates' soft skills, but what about your own ability to connect, empathize, and build rapport? Recruitment isn't just about matching skills to job descriptions—it's about shaping futures, and that takes more than just technical know-how. It requires a deep understanding of human behavior, emotional cues, and relationship-building.

Ask yourself:

How do you handle high-pressure situations, such as negotiating salaries or dealing with last-minute client changes?

Are you able to maintain composure when things get heated, or do your emotions sometimes get the best of you?

Can you consistently build trust and rapport with both candidates and clients, even during difficult conversations?

These questions aren't just self-reflection exercises—they're the foundation of becoming a more effective recruiter. According to the Harvard Business Review, recruiters with high EI make better hiring decisions and are more successful at navigating the complexities of human behavior (Goleman, 2017). Simply put, developing your own EI is essential for building stronger, more lasting connections in the hiring process.

READY FOR A REALITY CHECK?

So, if you're wondering why your efforts aren't getting the recognition you deserve, maybe it's time to put Emotional Intelligence front and center. Here's how you can start:

1. Self-Assessment & Awareness:

- Consider a recent interview where you felt particularly challenged. What emotions did it evoke, and how did you handle them?
- Ask for feedback from colleagues, mentors, or even candidates to understand how you come across emotionally.
- Use psychometric assessments to get a clear picture of your Emotional Quotient (EQ) and identify areas for growth.

2. Professional Development:

- Enroll in EI-focused coaching to strengthen your empathy, self-regulation, and communication skills.
- Attend workshops or seminars on emotional intelligence and body language to sharpen your interpersonal abilities.

3. Practice & Application:

- Next time you sense a candidate is nervous or hesitant during an interview, focus on making them feel at ease by acknowledging their concerns and adjusting your tone accordingly.
- Make empathy and active listening a priority in your daily interactions.

THE JOURNEY IS ONGOING

Developing Emotional Intelligence is not a one-off task; it's a continuous journey, but the rewards make every step worth it. Enhancing your emotional intelligence doesn't just improve your ability to work with people; it sets you up for long-term success in recruitment. When communication flows smoothly, relationships strengthen, and better decisions naturally follow.

Plus, you're fostering a workplace culture built on trust, collaboration, and shared motivation.

So why dive into this journey? It is because mastering Emotional Intelligence makes you indispensable not just to your candidates but to your clients as well. With EI, you transcend the role of recruiter; you become a leader, a trusted advisor shaping the future of talent acquisition.

As you sharpen these skills, you'll notice something magical—your professional network doesn't just grow wider; it grows deeper. Genuine trust and mutual understanding form the bedrock of these connections, taking your relationships beyond the transactional. This is where the real magic happens: when you're seen as more than just a recruiter, you become an invaluable asset to both your stakeholders, clients and candidates.

To guide you along this journey, use the template below to reflect on your experiences, track your progress, and identify areas for improvement. This structured approach will help keep you on course, ensuring that your Emotional Intelligence development stays front and center as you continue to evolve in your career.

Category	**Description**	**Example**
Date	*Record the date of the reflection.*	*April 20, 2024*
Interactions Recap	*Briefly describe key interactions of the day/week with candidates or colleagues.*	*Conducted a phone interview with a candidate who was approved. However, the candidate later requested a higher salary, exceeding the budget.*

Emotional Highlights	*Note any strong emotional reactions and what triggered them.*	*Felt frustrated when the candidate asked for a much higher salary after the offer was made.* ***Trigger:*** *Misalignment between expectations and budget.*
Impact of Emotions	*Reflect on how your emotions affected the outcome of interactions.*	*My frustration may have led me to dismiss the candidate's request without fully exploring their reasoning, possibly missing out on a valuable hire.*
Empathy Exercises	*Assess how well you understood and aligned with the emotions of others during these interactions.*	*Tried to understand the candidate's perspective on the salary request and reassured them that the offer was based on market analysis and internal equity.*
Self-Reflection	*Identify areas of strength and areas for improvement in managing your emotions.*	***Strength:*** *Managed to keep calm despite the candidate's sudden request.* ***Improvement:*** *Need to improve the ability to negotiate by showing empathy without feeling defensive.*

Action Steps	*List specific actions you will take to improve on the areas identified above.*	***Action 1:*** *Practice active listening and observe cues during salary negotiations. Focus on the candidate's tone and wording. When they raise concerns, acknowledge their feelings: "I understand that compensation is a priority for you, and I want to ensure we're fair." This will help build trust.* ***Action 2:*** *Identify cave points before entering negotiations. Decide what factors could lead to reconsidering the salary offer—perhaps internal flexibility or additional value the candidate brings. This ensures you stay open to adjustments without feeling rigid or defensive.*

Once you've enhanced your Emotional Intelligence, it's time to apply it to the hiring process. With resumes becoming more polished thanks to AI, finding the real potential behind the words requires a deeper understanding. This is where Emotional Intelligence becomes your secret weapon.

GET TO KNOW YOUR CANDIDATES

Some brutal honesty to make the day—today's job market is packed with candidates who have mastered the art of the perfect resume—thanks to Artificial Intelligence! They know exactly which buzzwords to use, how to highlight their experiences, and how to present their online presence in the best light possible. So, as a recruiter, how do you cut through the noise to find the real talent behind all that polish? It's more important than ever to dig deeper, ensuring you're not just filling a position but bringing in someone who will thrive and grow within the company.

Get the Description Right!

Here's the reality: It all starts way before you even meet the candidates. Crafting a strong, compelling, and accurate job description is the foundation for attracting the right talent. It's not just about listing responsibilities and qualifications; it's about painting a complete picture of the role, i.e., one that includes the core behaviors, soft skills, and cultural fit that truly matter. This sets the stage for better placements, stronger relationships between employees and employers, and, ultimately, a more harmonious workplace.

For example, let's say you're hiring for a Sales Manager role. Instead of just focusing on sales targets and industry experience, emphasize collaboration, adaptability, and emotional intelligence as key traits for success in the company culture. These aren't just buzzwords—they define the kind of talent that drives long-term growth and builds cohesive, high-performing teams.

For instance, consider the following example of a Sales Manager role:

<table>
<tr><td colspan="8">JOB DESCRIPTION TEMPLATE</td></tr>
<tr><td colspan="4">COMPANY NAME</td><td colspan="4">COMPANY LOGO</td></tr>
<tr><td colspan="2">JOB TITLE</td><td colspan="6">Sales Manager</td></tr>
<tr><td colspan="2">JOB POSTING</td><td colspan="6">☐ INTERNAL ☐ EXTERNAL ☐ BOTH</td></tr>
<tr><td colspan="2">JOB No</td><td colspan="3">[Insert Job No]</td><td>GRADE</td><td colspan="2">[Insert Grade]</td></tr>
<tr><td colspan="2">DEPARTMENT</td><td colspan="6">Sales & Business Development</td></tr>
<tr><td colspan="2">JOB LOCATION</td><td colspan="6">[Insert Location]</td></tr>
<tr><td colspan="2">REPORT TO</td><td colspan="6">[Insert Reporting Line Title]</td></tr>
<tr><td colspan="8">POSITION DETAILS</td></tr>
<tr><td>☐</td><td>FULL TIME</td><td>☐</td><td>PART-TIME</td><td>☐</td><td>HYBRID</td><td>☐</td><td>ON-SITE</td></tr>
<tr><td colspan="2">☐</td><td colspan="2">NEW POSITION</td><td colspan="2">☐</td><td colspan="2">BACKFILL POSITION</td></tr>
<tr><td colspan="4">TRAVEL REQUIRED</td><td colspan="4">BUDGETARY APPROVALS SECURED</td></tr>
<tr><td>☐</td><td>YES</td><td>☐</td><td>NO</td><td>☐</td><td>YES</td><td>☐</td><td>NO</td></tr>
<tr><td colspan="8">JOB OVERVIEW</td></tr>
<tr><td colspan="8">[Insert job overview]</td></tr>
<tr><td colspan="8">JOB SCOPE REQUIREMENT</td></tr>
<tr><td colspan="8">[Insert job scope requirement]</td></tr>
</table>

WORK EXPERIENCE REQUIREMENTS
[Insert work experience requirements]
EDUCATION REQUIREMENTS
[Insert education requirements]
CORE BEHAVIORS AND SKILLS
• **Adaptability:** Thrive in changing environments and quickly adjust strategies to meet new challenges. • **Problem-Solving:** Strong analytical abilities to identify and resolve issues efficiently. • **Influencing Others:** Effectively persuade and engage stakeholders to support sales initiatives and strategies. • **Negotiation:** Skillful in negotiating deals that achieve win-win outcomes for the company and clients. • **Communication:** Clear and persuasive communicator, able to convey ideas and strategies effectively. • **Competitive Drive:** Thrive in a competitive environment where continuous improvement and achieving excellence are paramount.

BACKEND OPERATIONS			
RECRUITER		**RECRUITMENT PANEL**	
EXPECTED HIRE DATE		**EXPECTED JOB POSTING DATE**	
ADDITIONAL COM-MENTS			

By including these emotionally intelligent traits in your job descriptions, you're setting the stage for candidates who are not just technically skilled but also aligned with the company's values and culture. These behaviors aren't just "nice to haves," but they are what separate good hires from great ones.

Now that you've crafted a more emotionally intelligent job description, it's time to dig deeper during the interview process. A polished resume can only reveal so much. Emotional Intelligence is where you separate those who can manage stress, collaborate effectively, and adapt quickly from those who merely possess technical skills. Here's how you can approach it:

Psychometric Assessment for Effective Hiring

So, how do you go beyond what's on the resume? Here's where psychometric assessments come in handy, e.g., tools like the EQ-i 2.0, developed by Reuven Bar-On. Now, this isn't about handing over your decision-making power as a recruiter to an algorithm. Instead, think of it as adding an extra layer of insight into the mix, giving you a clearer picture of a candidate's emotional intelligence.

The EQ-i 2.0, for instance, dives into areas like self-perception, stress management, and decision-making, which are critical emotional competencies that can often make or break a candidate's success at the workplace. While a resume might tell you about their technical prowess, these assessments help uncover the traits that determine how well they will handle challenges, collaborate with a team, or adapt to high-pressure situations.

When Emotional Intelligence is infused into every stage of Talent Acquisition, i.e., from job descriptions to final interviews, and you don't just hire for skills, you hire for long-term success.

Now that you've got the assessment data, it's time to validate it. Enter behavioral interviews—your opportunity to see EI in action. Let's break down why behavioral questions are your best ally in uncovering how candidates truly handle emotions under pressure.

Why Blend Psychometrics with Behavioral Interviews?

Let's be real: We've all been there, asking candidates the same typical questions during interviews and checking off boxes for skills and experience. But here's the thing: Traditional interviews often miss a crucial piece of the puzzle, i.e., **how** the candidate operates emotionally. In today's workplace, where soft skills and cultural fit are just as important as technical know-how, understanding how someone responds to challenges or connects with colleagues is essential.

While most interviews focus on the "what," i.e., what they've done and what skills they have, we often forget the "how," i.e., how they handle setbacks, how they manage stress, and how they build relationships with colleagues. Blended behavioral interviews dig into these key areas, revealing much about a candidate's emotional intelligence and how they might perform on the job.

The Problem with Traditional Questions

Let's cut to the chase: Traditional interview questions are stale. They're like asking someone on a first date, "So, what's your job?" instead of diving into what really makes them tick.

You get rehearsed answers, but do you really get to know the person? Not so much.

Here's the problem: "Tell me about your last job" or "What are your strengths and weaknesses?" These questions barely scratch the surface. They don't dig into how candidates handle stress, manage emotions, or navigate tricky workplace dynamics, which are all the things that truly matter when the pressure is on. You might end up hiring someone who looks great on paper, but without emotional intelligence, they could flounder when faced with real challenges.

It's like firing an arrow in the dark, hoping that the person's technical skills will be enough to get them through. Spoiler alert: They usually aren't.

But don't worry; there's a better way to figure out if someone has what it takes to thrive in your company. Psychometric assessments and behavioral interview questions offer a powerful combo that goes beyond surface impressions, giving you real insights into a candidate's emotional intelligence—a true game changer for long-term success.

Why Behavioral Interview Questions are a Game-Changer

If you want to dig deep into how someone actually *works*, not just what they've done, behavioral interview questions are your golden ticket. You're not asking hypothetical questions anymore, like, "How do you handle stress?" You're asking them to walk you through real-life situations: *"Tell me about a time when you were under serious pressure at work. What did you do?"* Now we're talking!

With questions like this, you can assess how they've handled tough situations before. **The goal?** To figure out how self-aware they are, how well they regulate their emotions, and how they connect with others when things get heated.

Here's what you should be looking for:

- **Self-Awareness**: Can they recognize their emotional triggers? Are they honest about their weaknesses and strengths?
- **Self-Regulation**: Do they keep their cool under pressure, or do they crack?
- **Empathy**: Can they read a room and adapt their communication style to others' needs?

These aren't just questions for leadership roles; every level can benefit from this approach. Whether you're hiring an entry-level employee or a seasoned executive, you'll get to the heart of who they are and how they'll fit within your team.

And that's where the magic happens. When you get past the resume and into real conversations, that reveals how a candidate will handle the ups and downs of your workplace.

IN A NUTSHELL

Behavioral interview questions are your go-to for diving into how a candidate really operates. These aren't the standard, surface-level queries—they're designed to make candidates dig deep and give you examples of how they've handled real-world emotional and interpersonal challenges.

Here's how to get to the heart of a candidate's emotional intelligence during interviews:

- **Self-Awareness**: "Tell me about a time when you received feedback that caught you off guard. How did you handle it, and what did you do next?"

IN A NUTSHELL

- **Self-Regulation**: "Share an example of when you reacted impulsively. What were the consequences, and how have you adjusted since then?"
- **Stress Management**: "Think back to a time when you were under significant pressure. How did you prioritize and maintain productivity?"
- **Empathy**: "Describe a time when you had to adapt your communication style to connect with someone whose perspective was very different from yours. How did you approach the situation?"
- **Adaptability**: "Tell me about a time when you faced a major change at work. How did you handle it?"
- **Interpersonal Skills**: "Give an example of a project where you had to work with a difficult team member. How did you manage the relationship to ensure success?"
- **Optimism**: "Describe a time when your workplace went through a big change, like restructuring or a management shift. How did you handle it?"

These questions aren't just for show. They help you get past the rehearsed answers and dive into how candidates really operate in the workplace, i.e., how they adapt, empathize, and thrive in the often-complex dynamics of a team. And that's where you find out if they'll be a great fit for your organization.

WRAPPING IT UP

At the end of the day, talent acquisition is about more than just ticking boxes on a resume. It's about seeing the whole person, i.e., seeing their emotional intelligence, how they handle pressure, how they connect with others, and how they align with your company's culture. The secret sauce to successful recruitment isn't just about skills; it's about emotional insight. When you blend EQ with the technical assessment, you're no longer just filling roles, but you're building thriving teams.

Remember, the candidates you bring on board today are the ones shaping your company's future. So, the next time you sit down for an interview, make sure you're not just asking the "what" but digging into the "how." Because that's where the magic happens—the place where resumes end and real connections begin.

Ready to step up your hiring game? It's time to recruit not just for today's needs but for tomorrow's potential.

CHAPTER HIGHLIGHTS

- **Importance of EI in Talent Acquisition:** EI plays a pivotal role in hiring, influencing not only technical skills but also a candidate's ability to thrive within the organizational culture.
- **Recruiter Self-Assessment:** Recruiters must reflect on their own EI to enhance relationship-building and make better hiring decisions.
- **Job Description Strategy:** Crafting job descriptions that integrate core behaviors and cultural insights is key to attracting candidates who are both technically proficient and aligned with company values.
- **Use of Psychometric Tools:** Use psychometric assessments that offer deeper insights into a candidate's emotional competencies, complementing traditional hiring methods.
- **Behavioral Interview Techniques:** Behavioral interviews focusing on past behaviors provide a clearer picture of a candidate's EI, aiding in selecting candidates who will excel in both the technical and emotional aspects of their roles.

References:

Cherniss, C. (2003). The role of emotional intelligence in organizational development. Emotional Intelligence and Organizational Effectiveness. Consortium for Research on Emotional Intelligence in Organizations. Retrieved from http://www.eiconsortium.org/reports/business_case_for_ei.html

Goleman, D. (2017). Emotional Intelligence: Why It Can Matter More Than IQ for Character, Health, and Lifelong Achievement. Bantam Books.

CHAPTER 5

EMOTIONAL INTELLIGENCE AND CONFLICT RESOLUTION

Think about it: What if our whole approach to emotions has been off base? We've been taught to "control" them, suppress them, or keep them in check as if emotions are a ticking time bomb. But what if we've been approaching it all wrong? What if, instead of trying to control emotions, we learned to listen to them and use them as signposts guiding us through tough situations?

Here's the truth: Emotions aren't the enemy. They're our internal compass, full of insight into what's happening beneath the surface, both within us and the people around us. Mastering them doesn't mean shutting them down; it's about understanding and using them to steer through challenges. And once you get the hang of it, conflict resolution takes on a whole new meaning.

WHAT ARE EMOTIONS?

Dr. Marc Brackett, an expert in the field, puts it simply: emotions are our brain's automatic reactions to internal or external events. They shape how we think, feel, and act (Brackett, 2019). Picture this: you're gearing up for a big presentation, and just before you start, the lights go out. Panic sets in—heart racing, palms sweating, mind spiraling with questions like "What now? What will everyone think?" That's your body's built-in fight-or-flight mode kicking into high gear, trying to protect you from perceived danger.

But here's where things can go off course: if we don'tunderstand these emotions, they can spiral out of control, leading to unnecessary conflict. We've all been there, right? Letting frustration or anger drive the conversation, only to regret it later. But what if you could step back and ask, "What's really going on here?" That's where Emotional Intelligence comes in.

Name It to Tame It

There's something almost magical about putting a name to what you're feeling. It's as if, once you identify the emotion, it loses some of its intensity. In fact, science backs this up, and there's a term for it: *Affect Labeling*. By simply naming your emotions, you begin to manage them more effectively (Torre & Lieberman, 2018).

Let's break it down with an example: You're in a meeting, and you feel a wave of frustration wash over you. But is it really just frustration? Or is it something deeper? Maybe you feel like your ideas aren't being heard, or worse, that they don't even matter. At first glance, the frustration is obvious, but underneath it might be a sense of being undervalued or ignored.

Once you've put a name to that deeper emotion–whether it's feeling sad, or afraid–you can start to deal with it. Instead of letting your frustration turn into passive-aggressive comments or, worse, an emotional outburst, you can address the core issue. You might say, "I feel like my input hasn't been fully considered, and I believe it adds value to the discussion." This way, you're opening up a conversation rather than creating a conflict.

The Power of Naming Emotions

Identifying your emotions isn't just a way to feel better. It completely changes how you approach challenges. When you take the time to pinpoint what's really going on, you're able to communicate more clearly and make decisions that defuse tension instead of escalating it.

It's all about clarity. Getting to the root of your emotions doesn't just calm you down; it helps you articulate your needs in a way that others can respond to constructively. You avoid the common trap of letting unspoken frustrations build up to resentment. Instead, you create an opportunity for real dialogue and resolution.

But there's more. When you name and express your emotions, you're not just identifying a reaction; you're choosing how to respond. This process puts you at a crossroads—you can choose vulnerability, inviting connection and understanding, or fall into the trap of victimhood, letting frustration and helplessness take the lead. By openly acknowledging what you feel, you reclaim control, creating the space for honest dialogue and meaningful resolution.

And it doesn't stop there. The ripple effect of this clarity touches every part of your professional life. Understanding your own emotional triggers sharpens your ability to read others' emotions, too. You become more adept at spotting when a colleague is stressed, when a client feels overwhelmed, or when a team member is holding back.

To help expand your emotional vocabulary, look at **Exhibit 5.1** below. It's a tool that helps you put precise words to your feelings so you can tackle them head-on. When you've got a full range of emotional labels at your disposal, you'll be better equipped to navigate even the most challenging situations with confidence and clarity.

Exhibit 5.1: Expanding Your Emotional Vocabulary

Primary Emotion	Expanded Labels
Angry	Irritated, Furious, Frustrated, Annoyed
Stressed	Overwhelmed, Pressured, Strained, Tense
Sad	Disappointed, Helpless, Hopeless, Upset
Anxious	Nervous, Worried, Afraid, Vulnerable
Hurt	Offended, Shocked, Jealous, Betrayed
Guilty	Ashamed, Regretful, Remorseful, Apologetic, Contrite

A Neuroscience Perspective

Let's take a look under the hood and see what's happening in the brain when emotions run wild. The prefrontal cortex, i.e., your brain's command center, is where all the magic happens. It's the part that helps you hit the pause button, weigh the consequences, and keep your cool when things start to heat up. This region is crucial for making rational decisions, especially under pressure.

But there's another player in the game, i.e., **the amygdala**, your brain's built-in alarm system. When it senses a threat, the amygdala hijacks your prefrontal cortex, sending you into fight-or-flight mode. Have you ever blurted out something in the heat of the moment and regret it later? That's your amygdala at work. It overrides your logical brain and pushes you to react impulsively.

The good news? Your brain is more adaptable than you think. Thanks to neuroplasticity, your brain's pathways can change and grow with the right practice. Mindfulness, deep breathing, and emotional intelligence training can help you rewire your brain so that the prefrontal cortex stays in control, even when emotions run high.

FROM UNDERSTANDING EMOTIONS TO MANAGING CONFLICTS

Here's the thing, our brains are wired to adapt, constantly reshaping and rewiring, thanks to neuroplasticity. And this is great news, especially when it comes to handling emotions during tense moments. Neuroplasticity means we are powered to train our minds to manage stress better, navigate tricky situations, and, ultimately, deal with conflicts in a smarter way.

But how does this play out in the real world, especially within diverse teams where cultures, personalities, and perspectives are constantly clashing and collaborating? Diversity is a goldmine for creativity and growth, but it also brings friction. This is where Emotional Intelligence becomes your superpower.

Rather than treating conflict as something to avoid, EI transforms it into an opportunity, i.e., a chance to bridge differences, find common ground, and create even stronger connections.

It's Not Just About Tit for Tat!

Picture this: A colleague makes a change in a project without looping you in, and suddenly, you're feeling all kinds of frustration. The instinct might be to snap back or get defensive, but is that really the best move? Conflicts, especially in teams, are rarely just about opposing opinions; they're about aligning different needs and perspectives. Instead of going head-to-head, emotional intelligence helps you shift the narrative from confrontation to collaboration.

Dr. Kenneth Thomas talks about effective conflict management as not just minimizing the bad but maximizing the good. When handled right, conflicts can be opportunities for growth and learning, not roadblocks. Emotional intelligence takes you from knee-jerk reactions to thoughtful responses that create harmony, not division.

The Silver Lining: From Friction to Function

Here's the upside: When you manage conflicts well, it can actually strengthen the team. Conflict, when managed with EI, doesn't just put out fires, but it sparks innovation and deepens team bonds. Imagine that instead of escalating tension, you're using those emotional smarts to foster understanding and collaboration. Suddenly, that friction? It's fuel for better teamwork and bigger breakthroughs.

Our instinct is to react when emotions run high, i.e., fight or flight kicks in, and it's easy to snap or shut down. However, what sets emotionally intelligent people apart is that they don't just react, but they respond. By taking a step back, understanding your emotions, and recognizing what's really driving the conflict, you are able to transform a potentially explosive situation into something constructive.

Mastering Conflict: EI Strategies You Can Use

Let's face it—conflict is part of every workplace. No matter how skilled or aligned a team may be, differences in opinions, personalities, and approaches are inevitable. But here's the good news: conflict doesn't have to be destructive. With the right Emotional Intelligence (EI) strategies, you can turn potential clashes into opportunities for growth, understanding, and even stronger connections. Here's how to master conflict in a way that brings out the best in you and your team.

Listen Beyond Words

Effective communication goes beyond simply exchanging words; it's about ensuring that listening isn't just hearing words but understanding the full message. Practice active listening by:

- **Tuning Into Non-Verbal Cues:** Body language often says more than words. Watch for gestures, posture, and facial expressions to get the full picture of what someone's feeling.

- **Engaging Actively:** Small signals like nodding or saying “I see” can show the other person that you're really present in the conversation.

Manage 'Amygdala Hijack':

The signs that you may have felt often, i.e., pounding heart, adrenaline rush, etc., indicate that the amygdala is hijacking your brain. Don't let it run the show.

- **Spot the Hijack**: Be aware of intense emotional signals like sudden anger or anxiety.
- **Regain Control**: Practice breathing techniques or take a brief pause to allow your brain's logical side to kick back in before responding.

Ask

Questions are powerful. They can clarify confusion and open up solutions.

- **Fact-Finding First**: Ask questions like “What's your perspective on this?” to get to the root of the issue without jumping to conclusions.

De-escalate Like a Pro:

When things heat up, have strategies ready to cool them down:

- **Use Calming Phrases**: Phrases like “Let's take a step back” or “I hear you” can help lower the emotional temperature in the room.
- **Try Breathing Exercises**: Techniques like the 4-7-8 method (inhale for 4 seconds, hold for 7, exhale for 8) can reduce stress instantly, helping you keep your cool.

Cultivate Empathy

It's not just about being nice; it's about truly understanding the other person's emotions and perspectives.

- **Step Into Their Shoes**: Try to see the conflict from their point of view. It changes the way you approach the conversation.

Use the "I" Statement

Instead of pointing fingers, express your feelings without blame.

- **Example:** Say, "I feel frustrated when meetings start late because it cuts into discussion time," instead of "You're always late."

Look for Win-Win Solutions

The resolution is not about winning or losing; it's about meeting everyone's needs.

- **Think Creatively**: Find a compromise that works for both sides by exploring all options, not just the obvious ones.

Reflect Before You React

Finally, embrace the mantra: "Think before you ink" before sending that fiery email or snapping in a meeting. Take a beat.

- **Pause & Process**: Even a few seconds to think can make the difference between escalating conflict or resolving it smoothly.

A WORD OF CAUTION

Let's be real. While **Emotional Intelligence** can be a game-changer for conflict resolution, it's not a one-size-fits-all solution. Sure, implementing EI strategies sounds great in theory, but HR and leadership need to tread carefully. If EI is applied with too much rigidity or a generic, cookie-cutter approach, it risks losing the very essence of what makes it powerful: its ability to support diverse perspectives and individual emotions.

The truth is that people don't all process emotions the same way. So, when you roll out EI training or conflict resolution strategies, they need to be adaptable, culturally sensitive, and personalized. Otherwise, you're setting yourself up for resistance or, even worse, surface-level compliance, where everyone *acts* emotionally intelligent without actually buying into the deeper principles.

Take personality differences, for example. If you try to apply the same conflict resolution method across the board without recognizing these unique traits, it's like trying to fit a square peg into a round hole. The result? Stiff interactions, missed emotional cues, and conflicts that never truly get resolved. Instead of fostering connection, you might end up stifling authentic emotional expression, i.e., completely missing the point.

So, what's the solution? HR and leadership need to strike a delicate balance. Emotional intelligence should encourage emotional growth but still respect individual differences. Thus change you create enables the birth of an environment where people feel heard, understood, and empowered, not just compliant. That's where the real magic happens.

CLOSING THOUGHTS

Here's the bottom line: We've been conditioned to suppress our emotions, but what if emotions are the secret sauce we've been ignoring all along? Instead of bottling them up, imagine if we actually *listened* to them. They're more than just reactions; they're signals guiding us through challenges, especially when tensions run high.

We can flip the script on conflict by simply harnessing emotional intelligence. Instead of letting conflicts break us down, we can use them to build better connections, create breakthroughs, and foster collaboration. So, the next time you're faced with a tense situation, remember that it's not about shutting down emotions; it's about *navigating* them with intention.

You've got the tools. You've got the insights. Now, it's time to put them all into action and turn every challenge into an opportunity for growth and understanding.

CHAPTER HIGHLIGHTS

- **Name It to Tame It:** Recognizing and labeling emotions is the first step to managing them effectively and preventing conflicts from escalating.
- **Affect Labeling:** Putting emotions into words can reduce their intensity, helping you navigate challenging situations with greater clarity.
- **Neuroscience and EI:** Understanding how the brain regulates emotions, particularly during conflicts, empowers you to respond thoughtfully rather than impulsively.
- **Turning Conflict into Growth:** Emotional intelligence allows you to transform conflicts into opportunities for team cohesion and innovation.
- **Practical Strategies:** Techniques like active listening, empathy, and reflective thinking are essential tools for resolving conflicts constructively.
- **HR's Role:** Effective application of EI in conflict resolution requires strategies that are adaptable, culturally sensitive, and considerate of individual differences.

References:

Brackett, M. A. (2019). Permission to Feel: Unlocking the Power of Emotions to Help Our Kids, Ourselves, and Our Society Thrive. Celadon Books.

Torre, J. B., & Lieberman, M. D. (2018). Putting Feelings Into Words: Affect Labeling as Implicit Emotion Regulation. Emotion Review, 10(2), 116–124. https://doi.org/10.1177/1754073917742706

Thomas, K. W. (2006). Conflict and negotiation processes in organizations. In W. C. Borman, D. R. Ilgen, & R. J. Klimoski (Eds.), Handbook of psychology: Industrial and organizational psychology (Vol. 12, pp. 889-919). John Wiley & Sons, Inc.

Edmondson, A. (1999). Psychological Safety and Learning Behavior in Work Teams. Administrative Science Quarterly, 44(2), 350-383. https://doi.org/10.2307/2666999

Goleman, D. (2017). Emotional Intelligence: Why It Can Matter More Than IQ for Character, Health, and Lifelong Achievement. Bantam Books.

CHAPTER 6

EMOTIONAL INTELLIGENCE AND LEADERSHIP EFFECTIVENESS

Global recessions and the looming fear of another economic downturn have pushed us to rethink leadership. Conversations within our professional network suggest that leadership is radically transforming, going from the traditional 'Yes-Boss' figures who have inherited positions to leaders with vigor, authenticity, and a growth mindset. These new leaders are self-aware, understand their limitations, and treat others with humility and respect.

Reflecting on our own experiences, we've all encountered different types of leaders who seem to have it all, i.e., sharp intellect, solid technical skills, and a deep understanding of their respective industries. Yet, despite these strengths, some struggle to truly connect with their teams and drive meaningful results. Conversely, there are leaders whose resumes may not scream 'rockstar,' yet they manage to bring out the best in everyone around them, regardless of their official leadership position. To us, it's equally important to remember that leadership is not just about vertical hierarchy. Contemporary leaders often work on a horizontal axis—those who challenge the status quo, those behind the scenes who make a difference, and those whose ideas and enthusiasm bring visions to life.

Still wondering what the secret ingredient is? Well, again, we say it is "*Emotional Intelligence,*" a quality rarely mentioned in job descriptions, performance reviews, or even during succession planning, yet it is crucial for leadership success.

Ultimately, we must acknowledge that the world needs more emotionally intelligent leaders. As they rise through the ranks, these leaders will be better equipped to overcome obstacles, communicate with influence, and understand that leadership is not a privilege for the few but a responsibility for those who can uphold it.

But why is emotional intelligence so crucial in this equation?

Because:

- It's the key to connection.
- It's what allows leaders to understand not just the task at hand but also the people behind the task.
- It helps them manage their own emotions while navigating the feelings of others, creating a more cohesive and motivated team.

Leaders, as decision-makers, act as the emotional compass for their organizations. Their emotions and reactions ripple through the team, setting the tone for either an innovative, vibrant environment or one weighed down by negativity. That's why we remind leaders to be mindful of the shadows they cast. Leaders who dwell on the negative can stifle creativity and motivation, while those who project optimism and resilience inspire confidence and enthusiasm, motivating their teams to tackle challenges head-on.

Winning the competition and riding the wave of continuous disruption, or the VUCA wave, requires a workforce powered by emotional intelligence to help reimagine the future, reignite engagement, replenish productivity, and ultimately call out for abundance in profitability.

THE SUBTLE POWER OF EMOTIONAL INTELLIGENCE IN LEADERSHIP

A reality check: every leader has tough and even tougher days, but the real difference lies in how they handle it. Leaders with high emotional intelligence do not allow a negative mood to derail the team's momentum. They're able to keep their emotions in check, maintaining a positive atmosphere, thus keeping everyone focused and motivated, no matter the levels of disruptions.

So, what really sets great leaders apart from the good ones? To begin with, we're witnessing a growing realization that true leadership goes beyond simply managing tasks. Leadership is about inspiring and guiding people.

To narrow this down, it's their ability to manage their own insecurities before focusing on their subordinates in the room. They embrace vulnerability and walk with poise and confidence while balancing both heart and mind in their communication. As the emotional compass of the organization, they navigate complexities with calmness and strategy.

This is not a theory; research backs it up. Daniel Goleman's work from the late '90s (Goleman, 1998) demonstrated that emotional intelligence is often a stronger predictor of leadership effectiveness than IQ. Further studies, like those by Cherniss (2001), show that leaders with high emotional intelligence drive better organizational performance, leading to higher employee satisfaction and profitability.

IN A NUTSHELL

What really makes a great leader?

Great leadership is a combination of the many intelligences crowned by emotional intelligence.

Great leadership is fueled by a genuine thirst for curiosity and the wisdom to assess what's known versus the unknown. It involves building capability through a growth mindset while understanding that diversity—both in people and cultures—plays a key role in leadership. Additionally, it's about taming the 'smartest person in the room' syndrome, where leaders learn to step back and encourage others to shine. It requires deep self-awareness, the courage to create psychologically safe environments, and the willingness to see different perspectives with empathy and compassion.

Without emotional intelligence, technical skills alone can fall flat, and team morale can suffer. It's worth pausing to reflect on this.

FROM INSTINCT TO INSIGHT

Caution! This may not sound English, and you may need to activate your prefrontal cortex!

Now this is not a surprise, but yet considered the best part! Mastering emotional intelligence is within everyone's reach, but it's not something that happens overnight. Those willing to transition from instinctual to insightful leadership consistently re-evaluate and refine their approach. Why? **Because they know leadership isn't just about doing; it's about being there.**

As we delve into some of the research done on our side and share some experiences witnessed through transitions by great leaders, we share tangible and succinct key steps they have adopted to help you evolve into the contemporary leader the modern world needs today:

- **Tune In To Your Emotions:** Start by recognizing and naming your emotions. When you feel something strong, pause and ask yourself: What triggered this? Is it external or internal? Understanding the source is the first step in managing emotions and engaging more empathetically with your team.
- **Seek Out 360-Degree Feedback:** Feedback is a powerful tool for growth, especially when it comes from all directions—peers, subordinates, and supervisors. Pair this with a 360-degree assessment to get a clear picture of how your emotional behaviors impact those around you. This process can uncover strengths you didn't know you had and, more importantly, reveal blind spots that might be holding you back. It's an invaluable step in both personal and professional development.
- **Practice Active Listening:** *We know that you know the drill, yet we will remind you still.* Listening isn't just about hearing words; it's about understanding the full message. Pay attention to the tone, watch for non-verbal cues, and respond thoughtfully. When you fully engage with the person speaking, you're not just hearing them; you're validating their feelings and perspectives. This kind of active listening fosters a culture of respect and open communication within your team.

- **Cultivate Empathy:** Try to see situations from others' perspectives, especially when conflicts or misunderstandings arise. Empathy doesn't just lead to better decision-making; it also builds stronger, more respectful relationships. Leaders who practice empathy connect on a deeper level, which enhances team cohesion and promotes collaborative problem-solving.
- **Maintain Healthy Emotional Boundaries:** Balancing boundaries is key to maintaining a healthy emotional climate. Know when to set limits to protect yourself from emotional burnout and when to open up to foster deeper connections. We are not associating this with hierarchy here. Those who master this balance create a positive atmosphere while keeping things professional, encouraging an environment where everyone can thrive. Don't try to handle everything on your own. Reach out to trusted colleagues or mentors when you need perspective or a sounding board. Sharing the emotional load can lead to more balanced decision-making and better emotional management overall.
- **Instill a Culture of Emotional Intelligence:** Developing your own emotional intelligence is just the beginning. As a leader, your behavior sets the tone for the entire team. You can create a workplace culture that values empathy, self-awareness, and effective communication when you personify and promote emotionally intelligent practices. When these behaviors are not just encouraged but celebrated, they become part of the organization's DNA.

Predominantly, this can be called the metamorphosis process of emotional intelligence excellence!

The art of leading with emotional intelligence means balancing personal and social competencies and knowing which to apply in each moment. This is what helps leaders navigate the complexities of the modern world.

The future of leadership isn't about who has the most ideas again; it's about who can bring out the best in others. Emotional intelligence isn't just another skill to add to the toolkit; it is "the toolkit". It's the subtle power behind every decision, the glue that holds teams together, and the driving force that leads organizations to success.

As you step back into your role, remember that leadership isn't about your title; it's about the positive impact you make on the lives of those you lead. The world needs contemporary leaders who can transition from instinct to insight, enhancing their presence and impact in the leadership arena.

As we conclude, we ask you to double down on your thoughts and to address your inner self on why you want to lead. Is it just to tick the box, or do you want to lead to save the bleed?

CHAPTER HIGHLIGHTS

- **Emotional Intelligence as a Leadership Differentiator**: EI is often what sets great leaders apart, enabling them to connect with and inspire their teams effectively.
- **Impact of EI on Team Dynamics**: Leaders with high EI shape a positive, resilient environment, influencing team morale and productivity.
- **Practical Steps for Enhancing EI**: Key strategies include tuning into emotions, seeking 360-degree feedback, practicing active listening, cultivating empathy, and maintaining healthy boundaries.
- **Leadership Shapes Organizational Culture**: Leaders who embody EI set the tone for a culture of empathy, resilience, and open communication.
- **The Future of Leadership**: Success in leadership hinges on the ability to elevate others through emotional intelligence, making it essential in today's dynamic world.

References:

Goleman, D. (1998). Working with Emotional Intelligence. Bantam Books.

Cherniss, C. (2001). Emotional intelligence and organizational effectiveness. In C. Cherniss & D. Goleman (Eds.), The Emotionally Intelligent Workplace: How to Select For, Measure, and Improve Emotional Intelligence in Individuals, Groups, and Organizations (pp. 3-26). Jossey-Bass.

Goleman, D. (2017). Emotional Intelligence: Why It Can Matter More Than IQ for Character, Health, and Lifelong Achievement. Bantam Books.

CHAPTER 7

EMOTIONAL INTELLIGENCE AND PERFORMANCE MANAGEMENT

You've just wrapped up your annual performance review. The process was the same as it's always been—structured, predictable, and based on a numerical rating system. Yet, as you leave the room, something doesn't feel right. You wonder whether the review truly captured your contributions or if it missed the mark, focusing more on outcomes than on the how—the behaviors, emotional intelligence, and interpersonal dynamics that make up so much of what you bring to the table.

This scenario is all too common. Traditional performance management systems, with their reliance on ratings and rigid metrics, often overlook the deeper aspects of what makes an employee truly effective. So, how can organizations turn this around?

The answer lies in integrating Emotional Intelligence into performance management.

While we won't overwhelm you with too many details about the common pitfalls of current organizational practices, some revealing data from Gartner is worth noting. A striking 86% of organizations still rely on ratings in their performance reviews, showing just how embedded this method is. Only a small portion, i.e., 5%, is even considering removing ratings soon, which suggests most organizations believe in their value. Additionally, 76% of companies conduct annual performance ratings, indicating a strong preference for regular, structured assessments of employee contributions.

But here's something to think about. 94% of organizations stress the importance of aligning employee behavior with company standards and values, but only 17% provide separate ratings for both outcomes and behaviors. This raises an important question: Are these performance evaluations truly capturing the full picture of an employee's contributions? (Gartner, 2022).

RECASTING PERFORMANCE MANAGEMENT

Despite advancements in technology and shifts in how we work, many organizations still rely on rigid and antiquated performance management practices. These methods often fail to engage employees and stifle opportunities for growth. So why do organizations hold on to them? Often, it's fear of change, concerns about resources, or analysis paralysis in the face of uncertainty.

Reflecting on our extensive industry experience, we know that performance reviews are more than just evaluations of pay and promotion; they affect an employee's engagement, sense of belonging, and self-worth. To truly motivate and retain top talent, organizations must move beyond rigid, outdated systems toward more dynamic, people-centric performance management methods. This shift not only recognizes the whole employee but also aligns performance strategies with the company's broader goals, fostering a more interconnected and engaged organizational ecosystem.

The key question is: "*How can performance management become more than a check-the-box exercise?*" "*How can it drive retention, win the war on talent, and transform your company into an industry leader?*" With no doubts, we say in rethinking how you design and apply these processes, making them your organization's ultimate competitive advantage—what we call your "serendipity carrot."

Well, what is a "serendipity carrot"? In short, it is those unexpected, fortunate outcomes that come from creating emotionally intelligent and people-centric processes. It's not just about dangling tangible rewards (as in the traditional "carrot" motivation model) but about fostering a work environment where performance excellence emerges naturally and where this only takes place when there's a deeper connection between organizational goals and individual contributions. This is ultimately a leeway for employees to feel truly valued, empowered, and motivated to succeed. How do you see this now as your true competitive edge?

From Rigid Systems to People-Centric Approaches

As we speak with global talent professionals, a common struggle emerges; they're working tirelessly to move away from one-size-fits-all performance frameworks, yet they often face resistance from senior leadership. This resistance can stem from fear of change or a lack of understanding about the benefits of more flexible systems.

Inspired by Simon Sinek's "Start With Why," we have concluded that the key to transforming performance management is rooted in purpose, i.e., what's in it for your people, your leaders, and your business. For transformations to be activated, a fundamental shift, like rebooting a system to restore optimal functionality, is profound. This approach prioritizes connection and communication over rigid metrics and fosters an environment where both leaders and employees can thrive.

We also believe that understanding the limitations of traditional methods is crucial for success. This means working toward shared authority over processes that are tailored to meet the unique demands of your organization today and tomorrow.

Multinational organizations are beginning to recognize that the conventional performance management systems—first popularized during World War II—are no longer fit for purpose. These outdated models, rooted in Frederick Taylor's "scientific measurement" approach, treat employees as cogs in a machine, stifling their potential for growth and creativity. The truth is that you can have the best talent, technology, and strategy, but if your teams don't trust each other, the system will fall apart. Performance management isn't just about metrics; it's about relationships. Leaders must create environments where trust, collaboration, and connection flourish.

Getting geeky and digging into research and beyond, we've asked ourselves the hard questions: why and how do traditional performance management systems fail? Research shows that conventional methods do little to improve effectiveness and may even erode employee morale (Cappelli & Tavis, 2016). Command-and-control leadership models, which these systems often support, reduce leaders to taskmasters and employees to passive participants.

These outdated frameworks often focus too heavily on weaknesses, causing leaders to overlook the strengths that could elevate the team. Standardized evaluations also fail to account for individual role differences, making comparisons unfair and distorting feedback.

The over-reliance on scoring mechanisms puts pressure on conformity, which stifles innovation. Ultimately, traditional performance management systems foster unhealthy competition rather than collaboration, and they often prioritize financial incentives over other crucial drivers of engagement, such as personal growth and development.

A New Approach to Performance Management

To modernize performance management, embracing transparency and adopting a coaching-based approach to feedback is a non-negotiable today for organizations. In reflection on our research on best practices, we share the following practical steps for ease and need for speed:

- **Frequent, Open Communication**: Shift away from annual reviews to regular, inclusive performance conversations. This could either at the moment through a gamified system or run more formal quarter-based systems, allowing a flow of continuous feedback and growth considering all cultural aspects.
- **Empower Employees with Tools**: Equip employees with the tools and how-to guides, as well as create employee resource groups that help them take ownership of their career progression with confidence. This in-

cludes self-assessment and reflection resources, access to skill development opportunities, mentorship, and perhaps reverse mentoring programs, too.

- **Forward-Looking Previews**: Move beyond reviewing past performance to include "previews" that focus on future potential. Yet a rich blend of both gives employees clear development pathways and actionable goals.
- **Real-Time Feedback Channels**: Expand feedback to allow for just-in-time input, ensuring that talent reviews and succession planning are informed by timely, relevant data.
- **Collaboration Over Competition**: Reframe reward systems from rigid pay-for-performance models to recognition-centered programs, away from the carrot and stick concepts that encourage personal growth and team collaboration.

By focusing on emotional intelligence and real-time feedback, performance management becomes a dynamic tool for employee development rather than a once-a-year evaluation.

WHAT DOES THE FUTURE FEARLESS LANDSCAPE LOOK LIKE?

Rather than overcomplicating things, we know the responsibility rests in the hands of the stakeholders involved. If there is a genuine desire to advance performance management, it requires transitioning from annual evaluations—those often-limited, one-off discussions—to fostering an environment where regular feedback thrives. This transformation can only be successful upon securing an "E-Motional" connect, where the head, heart, and hands are in synch, as well as when supported by high levels of emotional intelligence that have the Talent Management professionals ready for the debate-to-change, followed by intensive training programs on emotional intelligence as a skill across the board that ignites a more connected and purposeful mindset.

This shift leads to ongoing dialogue and continuous growth. While compensation teams may resist moving away from numerical ratings, employees will benefit from an approach that aligns individual aspirations with organizational goals, leading to boosted engagement and a higher sense of worth triumphing over success.

Let's be reminded: It is the 21st century, where performance management must evolve. The focus needs to shift toward continuous learning, fair rewards, and long-term development. Without these changes, organizations risk being left behind. Moving from traditional, rigid performance reviews to more dynamic, emotionally intelligent methods is essential for creating a thriving workplace.

To help visualize this transformation, **Figure 7.1** highlights the contrast between outdated, painful reviews and empowering, forward-looking performance previews. It shows how integrating emotional intelligence into performance management creates more effective, motivating feedback processes, ultimately leading to greater success for both employees and the organization.

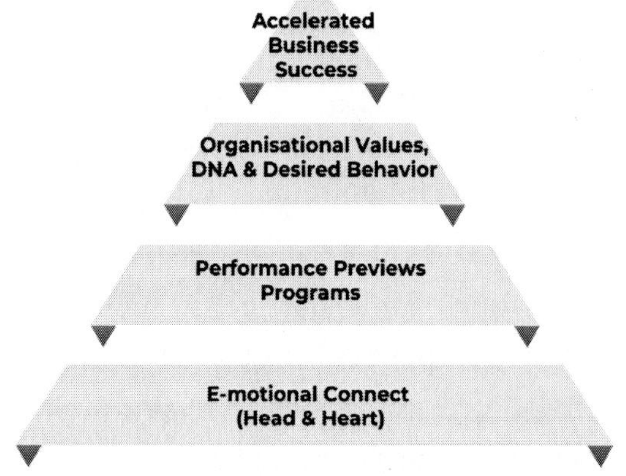

Figure 7.1: The daring conversation in regard to the conversion of painful performance reviews into powerful performance previews: A story to tell, inspired by Gemba Methodologies

Gemba Walks: A Revolutionary Approach

Imagine a new approach that takes leaders directly into the heart of the action, where they can connect with their people and see real-time performance. This is where **Gemba walks** come into play, revolutionizing performance management by immersing leaders in the day-to-day work environment.

Picture this: It's early morning at an automotive plant. The manager walks the floor, observing processes firsthand. Through open dialogue, they identify a minor delay in assembly, adjust, and immediately see improvements. But it doesn't stop there; the manager recognizes a standout employee on the spot, providing real-time, personalized feedback that boosts morale and reinforces a culture of collaboration.

The insights gathered during the Gemba walk feed directly into a digital performance system, adjusting goals and shaping employee development in real-time. This dynamic approach turns feedback from a static, backward-looking process into a living, breathing part of daily operations.

This is the future of performance management: engaged, connected, and constantly evolving.

FINAL THOUGHTS

The future of performance management belongs to leaders who master embedding Emotional Intelligence skills as they embrace real-time feedback while empowering their teams to become better and more resilient. Gemba walks, real-time feedback systems, and forward-looking performance previews aren't just new tools; they represent a fundamental shift toward a more dynamic, engaging, and people-focused approach. It is more like an omni-channel that is similar to "Drive-Through" concepts.

CHAPTER HIGHLIGHTS

- **Integrating EI into Performance**: Emotional Intelligence helps address the shortcomings of traditional performance management.
- **Key Statistics**: Despite dissatisfaction, **86% of organizations** still use ratings, and only **5%** consider removing them.
- **People-Centric Systems**: Shifting to dynamic, emotionally intelligent methods can create competitive advantages, such as higher retention and employee engagement.
- **Gemba Walks**: A real-time, immersive approach to performance management that fosters collaboration and immediate feedback.
- **Future of Performance**: Continuous learning, fair rewards, and emotional intelligence must be central to modernized performance systems.

References:

Cappelli, P., & Tavis, A. (2016). The performance management revolution. Harvard Business Review. Retrieved from https://hbr.org/2016/10/the-performance-management-revolution

Gartner. (2022). How organizations use performance ratings in employee evaluations. Retrieved from https://www.gartner.com

Sinek, S. (2009). Start with Why: How Great Leaders Inspire Everyone to Take Action. Penguin.

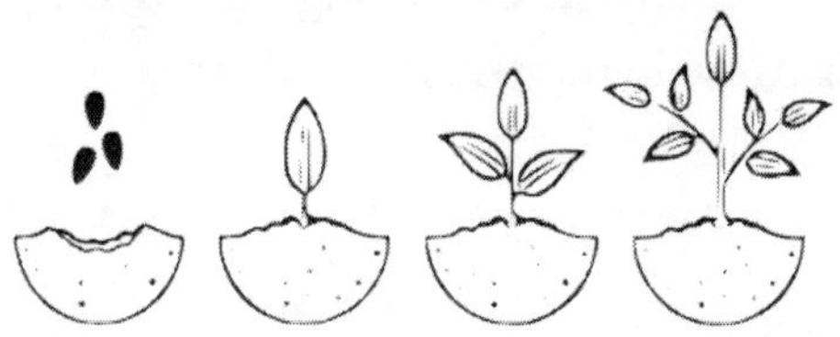

CHAPTER 8

EMOTIONAL INTELLIGENCE THROUGH LEARNING AND DEVELOPMENT

They say: *"A smart learning and development function strategizes and executes using emotional intelligence as the catalyst for success, creating not just a culture of learning but a learning culture."*

Let's break this down. In simpler terms, a proficient Learning and Development (L&D) function doesn't just focus on skill-building. It strategically uses Emotional Intelligence (EI) to shape an environment where continuous learning thrives. By recognizing the emotional dynamics within the workforce, L&D teams design training programs that not only educate but also truly engage employees on a deeper level. The key? Transparent communication, constructive feedback, and collaboration, all of which support professional growth while also building resilience and adaptability. The integration of EI in learning creates a sustainable culture that significantly boosts organizational performance.

In other words, it's about **bridging learning goals** with both **organizational** and **personal values**.

THE POWER OF EMOTIONAL CONNECTION

We've all been there, i.e., sitting through a training session packed with facts and figures, only to leave feeling disconnected. Why? Because while information is useful, without a human connection, it just doesn't stick. Research shows that up to 95% of training information can be forgotten—what we call "learning amnesia"—and the culprit is the lack of emotional engagement.

Emotional Intelligence is the real game-changer here. While technical expertise is important, teams thrive on empathy, collaboration, and resilience. These aren't just buzzwords; they are the factors that take a team from good to exceptional, and they are deeply influenced by EI. Today, EI is a necessity, not an option, in the realm of Learning and Development. We're shifting focus from technical skills to how people manage feedback, stress, and conflict, i.e., issues that deeply affect success.

Bringing this to life, perhaps you can consider a team member who possesses outstanding problem-solving abilities but falters under pressure or faces difficulties in interpersonal relationships. A true story while shopping at one of the luxury brands here in Dubai—tension rises, voices sharpen. It's a ticking time bomb. But before it could explode, an emotionally intelligent manager steps in. With calm empathy and composed leadership, they manage not just the customer but the entire emotional climate of the room. This wasn't about handling a difficult interaction; it was about understanding the emotions fueling it. And this is the power of emotional intelligence in action.

Now imagine this wasn't a one-off success story but the norm across your entire organization. Picture every manager and every team member effortlessly defusing tensions, fostering connections, and driving collaboration, all powered by emotional intelligence. This isn't a far-off dream; it's achievable when EI becomes an intrinsic part of your company's DNA.

So, how do you tattoo emotional intelligence into the heart of your organization?

Here's the real challenge: How do you take something as intangible as emotional intelligence and engrain it so deeply that it becomes second nature? This isn't about ticking off a box on your training checklist. Embedding EI requires a targeted, thoughtful strategy rooted in belief and perseverance. We call this approach **"seeing, feeling, and healing"**—the core of transformative change.

L&D teams play a pivotal role in carving emotional intelligence into the organizational framework. Through coaching, mentoring, and structured interventions, they can embed these essential skills, ensuring that emotional intelligence doesn't just exist in theory but thrives in everyday practice.

Here's a simple **three-step strategy** for embedding EI:

Surveillance: The Need for a Transformative Heart-Based Change

Embedding emotional intelligence starts by understanding your organization's emotional climate. Before diving into assessments or coaching, it's essential to **observe** the emotional dynamics shaping team interactions. This **surveillance phase** allows L&D professionals to identify underlying behaviors, attitudes, and emotional currents affecting both performance and communication.

By conducting this emotional landscape analysis, L&D teams, working closely with Chief Talent and Management Officers (CTMOs), can identify patterns that influence collaboration. This phase builds a **sense of urgency** around the need for emotional intelligence, and with sponsorship from leadership, a **guiding coalition** can champion EI as a core element of long-term success.

Assessments: The Jumpstart of a Transformative Journey

The next step? Self-discovery through assessments. Emotional intelligence can't just be "built on a whim"; it requires deliberate, strategic effort. These **psychometric assessments** offer individuals a personal roadmap for growth. But it's not just about the data; true progress happens when **coaching** translates these insights into real-world development. Here are some key assessments that help jumpstart this journey:

- **Bar-On Emotional Quotient Inventory (EQ-i):** Developed by Reuven Bar-On, this comprehensive self-report tool evaluates emotional and social functioning across 15 competencies grouped into five key areas: Self-Perception, Self-Expression, Interpersonal, Decision Making, and Stress Management. While the results are private to the individual, the EQ-i provides a well-rounded view of emotional intelligence, offering insights that individuals can use to guide their personal and professional growth (Bar-On, 2006).

- **Mayer-Salovey-Caruso Emotional Intelligence Test (MSCEIT):** Created by Peter Salovey, John Mayer, and David Caruso, the MSCEIT measures emotional intelligence as a set of cognitive abilities. It assesses four critical areas: perceiving emotions, using emotions to facilitate thought, understanding emotions, and managing emotions. Although individual results remain private, the MSCEIT helps individuals understand their emotional capabilities, offering a foundation upon which they can build through targeted training (Mayer, Salovey, & Caruso, 2002).
- **Schutte Self-Report Emotional Intelligence Test (SREIT):** The SREIT, also known as the Schutte Emotional Intelligence Scale, is a straightforward self-report inventory that assesses core aspects of emotional intelligence, such as emotional perception, regulation, and utilization. This tool is designed to be simple and accessible, giving individuals a quick yet meaningful gauge of their emotional intelligence, which they can use to focus their personal development efforts (Schutte et al., 1998).

Together, these tools provide more than just numbers; they reveal strengths and areas for growth, allowing L&D professionals to create **tailored interventions** that drive change.

Coaching: The catalyst for transformation

Understanding your emotional intelligence is one thing, but using it effectively is where the transformation happens. This is where coaching steps in, turning insights into actionable development. Coaching is the bridge between theory and practice, offering a personalized roadmap for applying emotional intelligence in real-life scenarios.

- **Personalized Development Plans**: Coaching helps individuals craft development plans that align with their specific EI goals, addressing challenges identified in the assessments.
- **Ongoing Support and Accountability**: Continuous support ensures that individuals stay on track. Regular feedback sessions help adjust strategies as necessary.
- **Practical Application**: Coaching focuses on applying EI skills in real-life situations, whether managing stress or improving communication.

While coaching provides the framework, true change occurs when these practices are consistently applied in everyday work. It's about moving from knowledge to **action**, making emotional intelligence a tangible part of your organizational culture.

TURNING KNOWLEDGE INTO ACTION

Knowing about emotional intelligence is just the first step; living it is where the magic happens. When emotional intelligence is truly integrated into daily interactions and team dynamics, L&D teams can confidently say that EI isn't just a buzzword but a living, breathing part of the organization's DNA.

- **Start with What's Missing:** Identify the emotional intelligence gaps your team needs most. Is decision-making under pressure a weak spot? Focus on stress management and emotional regulation. *Increase urgency.*
- **Set Clear, Actionable Objectives:** Define what success looks like. Is your goal to enhance team communica-

tion? Focus on building empathy and active listening skills that directly tackle everyday challenges. *Get the vision right.*

- **Use the Right Tools:** Tailor your exercises to your objectives. Want to build assertiveness? Role-playing scenarios can be highly effective. Need to boost self-awareness? Try activities like the Ripple Effect to show how emotions ripple through teams. *Get the buy-in and empower action.*
- **Launch with Intention:** Roll out your program with clear goals. Make sure participants know what's expected and why it matters. A well-planned launch sets the tone for real impact. *Make short-term wins.*
- **Adapt Along the Way:** Keep an ear to the ground; gather feedback after each session and tweak where necessary. This loop of improvement keeps the program relevant and effective. *Don't let up.*
- **Measure What Matters:** Don't just rely on assumptions. Look for real improvements. Have conflicts decreased? Are people managing emotions better? These are the signs of emotional growth. *Make the change stick.*

Embedding emotional intelligence development into your organization is powerful because it is flexible and customizable, i.e., it can be tailored to your team's specific needs. Once it is in the DNA of your organization, it becomes second nature.

TOPICS AND CONTENT IDEAS

Here's the thing: Building emotional intelligence isn't just about ticking off boxes or teaching skills; it's about making it part of everyday actions. When emotional intelligence is woven into how we work and connect, it's not just another leadership trend; it becomes the heartbeat of your organization. So, how do you make that shift?

Daniel Goleman's four core areas of emotional intelligence—Self-Awareness, Social Awareness, Self-Management, and Relationship Management—form the bedrock of this transformation. But how do you bring these concepts to life in a way that sticks? Here's how you can take these ideas from theory to practice and infuse them into your daily workplace culture:

Self-Awareness: The Starting Point for Leadership

Have you ever witnessed someone lose their cool during a meeting? That's where self-awareness comes into play—understanding our emotional triggers is the bedrock of great leadership.

- **Thought/Behavior Diaries:** Encourage employees to keep track of their emotional reactions throughout the day. This allows them to notice patterns, whether it's stress before presentations or frustration during feedback.
- **Mood Tracking:** With apps or simple journals, team members can record their moods, leading to clearer self-awareness about what triggers both positive and negative emotional responses.

Social Awareness: Tuning Into Others

It's not just about you; it's about how well you can tune into the emotions of those around you. Social awareness is critical to understanding the dynamics within a team.

- **Role-Playing Exercises:** Challenge your team with scenarios that require reading social cues. Role-playing situations like giving tough feedback or handling a stressed colleague help sharpen these skills.
- **Workshops on Non-Verbal Communication:** Non-verbal cues like body language are often more telling than words. Workshops that focus on interpreting facial expressions, tone, and gestures can dramatically enhance social awareness.

Self-Management: Handling the Pressure

Are you staying composed under pressure? It's a skill and one that can be taught. Self-management is about regulating emotional reactions so they don't derail your performance.

- **Stress Management Techniques:** Teach your team mindfulness techniques such as deep breathing or progressive muscle relaxation. These practices help individuals maintain their composure during high-stakes moments.
- **Emotional Regulation Case Studies:** Provide real-world scenarios where emotional management was key to success. Use these to guide team discussions and help them practice staying emotionally composed.

Relationship Management: Building Strong, Trusting Teams

People perform their best when they feel connected. Relationship management is about fostering empathetic relationships that help teams communicate and collaborate more effectively.

- **Empathy Exercises:** These could include listening exercises where team members reflect on what they heard or storytelling sessions to understand different perspectives. The goal is to build a culture of empathy.
- **Constructive Feedback Workshops:** Giving feedback can be tough. Teach your team how to deliver constructive feedback that is both respectful and growth-oriented. This not only helps individuals grow but also strengthens the trust within the team.

And there's more to the equation. To truly make emotional intelligence stick, you need to tap into the science behind it and turn conflicts into opportunities for growth:

Brain and Neuroscience: Understanding Emotional Triggers

Why do we react the way we do? A basic understanding of the brain's emotional processes can be a game-changer for your team.

- **Explaining Emotional Reactions:** Show employees how the limbic system, which controls emotions, and the prefrontal cortex, responsible for decision-making, interact. Understanding this connection helps individuals manage emotional impulses more effectively.
- **Neuroplasticity for Change:** Explain the concept of neuroplasticity, i.e., the brain's ability to rewire itself through repeated behaviors. This helps team members realize that personal change is not only possible but sustainable through consistent effort.

Conflict Management: Turning Tension into Collaboration

Tension isn't necessarily a bad thing. If managed correctly, it can lead to growth and stronger teams. Emotional intelligence plays a vital role in managing conflict productively.

- **Conflict Resolution Skills Training:** Help employees learn negotiation tactics and problem-solving techniques that lead to win-win situations. When team members can resolve disputes constructively, the entire team benefits.
- **Role-Playing Conflict Scenarios:** Create simulations where participants must resolve disputes under pressure. This real-time practice builds confidence in navigating difficult conversations and turning conflicts into collaborative opportunities.

By integrating these topics into your development sessions, you're not just imparting knowledge—you're cultivating a culture where emotional intelligence becomes second nature. Even in volatile, uncertain, complex, and ambiguous (VUCA) environments, emotional intelligence will anchor your team, driving them toward consistent, thoughtful actions.

FINAL THOUGHTS

Here's the reality: Emotional Intelligence isn't just another skill; it's the foundation of a **connected, thriving workplace.** Designing an emotional intelligence development program with purpose means you're doing more than teaching people how to manage their emotions. You're shaping a culture rooted in empathy, resilience, and collaboration.

Sure, the transformation won't happen overnight, but when you commit to embedding emotional intelligence in your organization, the long-term payoff is extraordinary: stronger teams, healthier communication, and a more engaged workplace. That's the kind of shift that not only sticks but it transforms.

Now, isn't that the future of work we all want?

CHAPTER HIGHLIGHTS

- **Emotional Intelligence is the Catalyst for Success:** EI is what transforms teams from simply functional to thriving. It fosters collaboration, enhances productivity, and builds a resilient, connected work environment.
- **Start with Self-Awareness:** Knowing where you stand emotionally is the foundation for growth. Assessments like EQ-i and MSCEIT provide a roadmap for developing emotional intelligence.
- **The Role of Coaching:** Insights from assessments are just the beginning. Coaching takes these insights and turns them into personalized, actionable development plans that drive real-world change.
- **Effective EI Development Strategies:** To make emotional intelligence development stick, identify specific gaps, set clear, actionable goals, use practical tools like role-playing and group discussions, and continuously adapt the program to your team's needs.
- **Focus on Core EI Competencies:** The most impactful EI programs enhance Self-Awareness, Social Awareness, Self-Management, and Relationship Management—building stronger individuals and teams.

CHAPTER HIGHLIGHTS

- **Sustained Benefits for Your Organization:** Integrating EI development into the fabric of your organization fosters long-term success. Teams that practice EI are more adaptable, communicative, and effective, leading to a lasting positive impact on organizational culture.

References:

Bar-On, R. (2006). The Bar-On model of emotional-social intelligence (ESI). Psicothema, 18(suppl), 13-25.

Goleman, D. (1995). Emotional Intelligence: Why It Can Matter More Than IQ. Bantam Books.

Kotter, J. P. (2007). Leading change: Why transformation efforts fail. In Museum management and marketing (pp. 20-29). Routledge.

Mayer, J. D., Salovey, P., & Caruso, D. R. (2002). Mayer-Salovey-Caruso Emotional Intelligence Test (MSCEIT): User's manual. MHS Publishers.

Pollack, J., & Pollack, R. (2014). Using Kotter's eight stage process to manage an organisational change program: presentation and practice. Systemic Practice and Action Research, 28(1), 51–66. https://doi.org/10.1007/s11213-014-9317-0

Schutte, N. S., Malouff, J. M., Hall, L. E., Haggerty, D. J., Cooper, J. T., Golden, C. J., & Dornheim, L. (1998). Development and validation of a measure of emotional intelligence. Personality and Individual Differences, 25(2), 167-177.

CHAPTER 9

BONUS CHAPTER - HOW TO GIVE FEEDBACK WITH EMOTIONAL INTELLIGENCE

Giving feedback can sometimes feel like walking a tightrope. And if we're being honest, receiving it can feel even trickier. But what if we flipped the script? When you bring Emotional Intelligence into the mix, feedback stops being a source of tension and turns into a chance for real connection and growth. It's not just about pointing out what's wrong; it's about paving the way for stronger relationships and personal development.

We touched on this back in Chapter 5, i.e., emotions aren't just fleeting moments; they're at the core of how we interact with each other. If you feel like ignoring or pushing them down, it only leads to more problems. The tension doesn't just disappear; it simmers, building up until it eventually explodes. As Smith and Doe (2024) pointed out, when you use emotions wisely, they become the key to more authentic conversations. Think of feedback as a chance to *connect* rather than *correct*.

"It's about connection, not correction."

Let's talk about those nerve-wracking conversations we've all had—breaking the news to a dedicated team member that they didn't get the project or addressing someone whose recent behavior has been stirring up the team dynamic. It's natural to feel anxious. We dread these conversations because we fear conflict, backlash, or hurting someone's feelings.

But here's the kicker: feedback triggers more than just emotional reactions. It can also set off physical responses like sweaty palms and a racing heart that twists in your stomach. Our fight-or-flight instinct kicks in, making it even harder to stay cool and collected. Yet, emotional intelligence is the secret sauce for navigating these tricky moments. You're not there to criticize; you're there to connect, help someone grow, and ultimately make the team stronger.

MASTERING THE ART OF DIFFICULT CONVERSATIONS

Let's face it: Difficult conversations are part of the job. Whether it's addressing a performance issue or diving into a sensitive topic, these moments challenge your emotional intelligence. Here's how to master them:

See Something, Say Something

Don't let small issues snowball. If someone is repeatedly late, don't sit on it; rather, address it directly. For instance, if a team member is often late, address it directly: "*I've noticed you've been late a few times this week. Let's talk about what's going on and how we can fix it.*" This keeps the issue relevant and manageable.

In-Person Over Email

Whenever possible, give feedback face-to-face. Body language speaks volumes, and you can build more trust in the person. Instead of shooting off an email, say, "*Can we chat about your recent project?*" That personal touch makes all the difference.

Prepare with Purpose

Think about what you want to achieve from the conversation. If a deadline was missed, frame it as a learning opportunity and say, *"Let's figure out what went wrong and how we can prevent it in the future."* This keeps the focus on growth, not blame.

Encourage Dialogue, Not Monologue

Make feedback a two-way street. If a project didn't hit the mark, ask, *"How do you feel it went? What worked and what didn't?"* This invites their perspective and fosters a more balanced conversation.

Replace the Feedback Sandwich

We've all heard of the "feedback sandwich" (praise, critique, praise), but let's be honest—it waters down the message. Instead, be straightforward: *"Your report was thorough, but with more practice, your presentation could match that level."* Clear, actionable stand and no sugarcoating.

Listen More

In tough conversations, *listening* is your most powerful tool. If someone's struggling, start with, *"How are things going? What's been challenging for you?"* By listening first, you'll understand their perspective and avoid jumping to conclusions.

Foster Openness

Make it clear that feedback is a collaborative process. If someone's having trouble with a tool, try, *"I've noticed you're having some challenges with this software. Let's figure it out together."* This takes the defensiveness out of the conversation.

Promote Problem-Solving Together

Instead of offering all the answers, invite them to find solutions. If deadlines are slipping, ask, *"What do you think would help you manage time better?"* Giving them ownership makes them more invested in finding a fix.

Fail Forward

Share your own experiences with setbacks. For example: *"I remember struggling with time management earlier in my career. Let's see what we can learn from this experience."* This fosters resilience and shows that failure is part of growth.

Be Vulnerable

Admit when you could have done better. If something went wrong, say, *"I realize I could've provided more direction. Let's work on improving that together."* Vulnerability builds trust and strengthens relationships.

These strategies turn feedback from something people *dread* into something they can *embrace*. It's about creating a culture of growth and openness.

A WORD OF CAUTION

Of course, not all feedback conversations go smoothly. When mishandled, they can have ripple effects that damage teams. Here's what to watch out for:

- **Emotional Spirals**: If the conversation goes off track, emotions can snowball. What started as a small issue might blow up, making it hard to find a resolution.
- **Defensiveness and Blame**: Without empathy or structure, things can quickly devolve into finger-pointing, leaving both parties feeling attacked rather than helped.
- **Broken Trust**: Mishandling a sensitive topic doesn't just cause tension at the moment; it erodes trust. Future conversations become more difficult because people start putting up walls.
- **Resentment and Disengagement**: Poor feedback management can lead to frustration. Over time, this can turn into disengagement, with team members pulling back and contributing less.

Final Thoughts

At the end of the day, feedback isn't about pointing fingers; it's about building bridges. With empathy, self-awareness, and a genuine desire for growth, feedback becomes less of a minefield and more of an opportunity for collaboration. And here's the thing:

Mastering emotionally intelligent feedback is an ongoing practice. It's about *showing up*, listening, adapting, and being authentic in every conversation.

It takes time to develop these skills, but the payoff? It's huge. When feedback is delivered with emotional intelligence, trust deepens, performance improves, and your team thrives. So, don't shy away from tough conversations. Embrace them with openness and vulnerability, and watch as your workplace shifts from one of fear and defensiveness to a space of collaboration and growth. In the end, it's not just *what* you say; it's *how* you say it and the connection it fosters.

CHAPTER HIGHLIGHTS

- **Feedback with Emotional Intelligence:** Approach feedback as an opportunity for growth, understanding, and stronger relationships by balancing self-awareness, empathy, social awareness, and clear communication.
- **Navigating Difficult Conversations:** Emotional intelligence helps manage high-stakes conversations by reducing anxiety, maintaining composure, and fostering understanding.
- **Key Strategies for Effective Feedback:** Speak up early, opt for face-to-face discussions, prepare with intention, encourage dialogue, and replace the feedback sandwich with direct, supportive communication.
- **Importance of Listening:** Active listening is crucial during tough conversations, helping to uncover underlying issues and build trust.
- **Fostering Openness and Collaboration:** Engage in two-way dialogue, promote problem-solving together, and embrace vulnerability to strengthen team dynamics.
- **Common Pitfalls:** Be aware of the risks of poorly managed conversations, such as heightened emotional reactivity, defensiveness, and erosion of trust.
- **Continuous Improvement:** Feedback is an ongoing process—cultivate a culture of learning and emotional intelligence to ensure long-term team success.

References:

Goleman, D. (1995). Emotional Intelligence: Why It Can Matter More Than IQ. Bantam Books.

Smith, J., & Doe, R. (2024). Understanding and Managing Emotions in the Workplace. Organizational Behavior Press.

*Torre, J. B., & Lieberman, M. D. (2018). Putting Feelings into Words: Affect Labeling as Implicit Emotion Regulation. *Emotion*, 18(3), 424-443.*

CHAPTER 10

NAVIGATING THE FUTURE WITH EMOTIONAL INTELLIGENCE

We're standing on the edge of a workplace revolution. The future of work? It's not just about what we do—it's about how we *connect* and *adapt* in an ever-evolving world. Technology is advancing at warp speed. Artificial Intelligence (AI), automation, and digital tools are changing the landscape of nearly every industry. But here's the twist: no matter how sophisticated the machines get, they'll never replicate the one thing that makes us *human, i.e.,* Emotional Intelligence.

Think about it. AI might crunch data and handle routine tasks, but can it understand the subtle nuances of a conversation? Can it show empathy, build trust, or inspire a team? Not quite. And that's exactly why emotional intelligence will be the ultimate differentiator in the future of work. The things that make us uniquely human—empathy, creativity, and the ability to navigate complex social interactions—are the skills that will keep us relevant and in demand.

According to the World Economic Forum (2020), emotional intelligence is no longer just a "nice-to-have" skill. It's essential. In fact, as automation takes over routine tasks, soft skills—like problem-solving, emotional understanding, and people management—will become the *real* game-changers. The bottom line? Technology may change how we work, but emotional intelligence will determine *who* leads the future.

THE FUTURE NEEDS A HUMAN TOUCH

Let's cut to the chase: mastering the latest tech is important, but here's the thing: it's not enough. While AI can automate processes and optimize efficiency, it can't lead with compassion or inspire genuine connection. That's where emotional intelligence steps in. The leaders of tomorrow won't just be tech-savvy. They'll be emotionally intelligent, capable of connecting with their teams on a deeper level and leading with empathy, adaptability, and vision.

In a world where everything is going digital, the human touch becomes more valuable than ever. We're talking about leaders who can create inclusive work cultures, managers who understand that their people are more than just productivity metrics, and teams that thrive on collaboration and connection. Emotional intelligence isn't just a skill; it's the *heart* of effective leadership in the future.

Here's a thought: Technology may run the operations, but emotional intelligence drives *real* success. Leaders who understand that technology is a tool, not the endgame, are the ones who will rise to the top. They'll use their emotional intelligence to build relationships, foster innovation, and manage change with grace. Because when things get tough, it's not the machines that people turn to; it's their leaders.

Ask Yourself This:

As AI takes over more tasks, are you using technology to enhance your humanity or replace it? The future demands that we lean into our uniquely human qualities, like empathy, creativity, and emotional intelligence, because these are the traits that will help us thrive in a world dominated by data and automation.

Imagine this: In a sea of automation, *your* humanity becomes your superpower. It's not about keeping pace with machines; it's about doing what machines *can't*. Empathy can't be coded, creativity can't be automated, and true connection can't be programmed. That's why, no matter how advanced technology gets, emotional intelligence will always be your most valuable asset.

Balancing Tech and Humanity

The real question isn't whether we need AI. It's how we balance it with our human touch. The future of work isn't just a race to adopt the latest technologies; it's about learning how to harness these tools to enhance human connection. Leaders who can strike this balance will create work environments that are both efficient and deeply connected, where teams are inspired, not just managed.

Example: Think of AI as a co-pilot. It can guide the flight, but it's the human pilot who makes the final call, especially when emotions, relationships, and well-being are at stake. So, as we build our future alongside AI, we must remain firmly rooted in the emotional skills that make us irreplaceable.

FINAL THOUGHTS: LEADING WITH HEART IN A DIGITAL WORLD

In this ever-evolving landscape, the leaders who will thrive are those who never lose sight of their humanity. It's about more than just implementing new systems or optimizing processes; *it's about leading with heart.* As technology accelerates, emotional intelligence will ensure that we stay grounded, connected, and human.

Think about it this way: in a world overloaded with information and automation, the ability to connect on a human level will be your competitive edge. The future belongs to those who can blend the brilliance of technology with the depth of emotional intelligence. It's about knowing when to leverage AI and when to lean into the human touch. That's the sweet spot where innovation meets empathy and where leaders not only *survive* but *thrive.*

References:

World Economic Forum. (2020). The Future of Jobs Report 2020. Geneva: World Economic Forum. Retrieved from https://www.weforum.org/reports/the-future-of-jobs-report-2020

Made in United States
Cleveland, OH
22 January 2025

13689578R00087